DISCIPLING
MIDDLE EASTERN
BELIEVERS

RAY G. REGISTER, JR. DMin

GlobalEdAdvancePress
37321-7635 USA

DISCIPLING MIDDLE EASTERN BELIEVERS

Library of Congress Control Number: 2009931518

Register, Ray G., Jr. 1935–
Discipling Middle Eastern Believers

ISBN 978-1-935434-36-8

Subject Codes and Description: 1: REL03700:
Religion: Islam – General; 2: REL037030: Religion:
Islam – Rituals & Practice; 3: SOC048000: Social
Science: Islamic Studies.

Printed in the United States of America

Cover design by Barton Green

Published by

GlobalEdAdvancePress
37321-7635 USA

TABLE OF CONTENTS

INTRODUCTION

When I first started relating to Muslims and studying Islam, the major question among Evangelical Christians with a heart for the Islamic world was, "Can Muslims really come to the Lord?" We were taught by great scholars and Islamicists like Dr. Kenneth Cragg to exercise patience in our interfaith witness with Muslims. Today, after almost 40 years, the relevant question is, "How does a Muslim background believer grow in Christ?" A resurgence of fanatical Islam has brought about catastrophic world events. At the same time, a growing number of Muslims are becoming believers in Jesus in every Islamic country. The sowing of the good news of salvation in Jesus is reaping a harvest in the midst of persecution and turmoil. This book is a sequel to my first on "Dialogue and Interfaith Witness with Muslims."[1] It addresses the observation of the late Dr. Elmer Douglas, my professor of Islamic Studies at Hartford Seminary Foundation, that, "The question is not whether Muslims can come to Christ, but what do we do with them after they become believers in Him?" He, as many others working in Muslim countries, had faced the difficulties of the Muslim believer in Jesus in dealing with the hostility of his own Muslim culture, and the lack of welcome into the existing Christian community.

I therefore share the following observations and experiences in trying to disciple Muslim background believers in Jesus with the hope and prayer that they may be helpful to all who work in and pray for the Muslim world. Our goal and expectation is that you may see the living Christ shape your Muslims friends into his image. I must admit my own limitations in that the majority of my experience has been with Sunni Muslims of Palestinian origin who live in or once lived in the

Holy Land. Many are men who, though oral communicators, can read and write. An excellent resource for working with Muslim women who are oral communicators and often involved in occult practices is "**Ministry to Muslim Women, Longing to Call Them Sisters**" which is a compendium of over 40 women who worked among Muslim women worldwide.[2] The most candid and sympathetic description of these Muslims is by Professor Bill Baker in his recent book, **Arabs, Islam and the Middle East**.[3] A Muslim from Jordan shares his personal testimony of faith in **The Man from Gadara. The Camel Training Manual** provides a practical approach to discipling Muslims. Caring for converts from Islam is emphasized in **Welcome Home.** The groundbreaking work in **Servants in the Crucible,** provides invaluable insights from 450 interviews with Muslim background believers and others. Roy Aksnevad has written an insightful paper on **Leadership Development Within the Mbb Community** based on a survey of North American believers.[4]

I have had some limited experience with Muslims from other areas of the Middle East and around the world. I apologize to you and to my Muslim friends for what may appear to be stereotypes. Muslim background believers in Jesus are from every nation of the world and represent a wide variety of economic, education and social groups. Each has his or her individual personal experience with the Lord. It would be naïve to think that one approach fits every Muslim. On the other hand, all Muslims are part of a family, tribe, sub-culture and the Nation of Islam. Therefore, some of what I share about discipling, mentoring and counseling Muslim background believers will have application to all Muslims. I must make clear the use of terminology. I call a Muslim who has trusted Jesus Christ as personal savior from his sins, a "Muslim background believer" or Mbb. They would be considered in the C4-C5 Spectrum with a few in C6 as described in Appendix 5. He or she is still a Muslim by culture. They are not "Christians" in the cultural sense any more than a Jewish Messianic believer in Jesus is a "Christian." Many Jewish Messianic friends protest vehemently if we call them Christians. Even though they have found the fulfillment of the Scriptures in Jesus their Messiah, they have not entered the Gentile world of Christians emotionally or culturally. Many still observe the Jewish Sabbath, attend Messianic synagogues, and observe the Jewish feasts. Most Muslim background believers, especially the first generation whom we are dealing with, still live in Muslim families and Muslim cultures. They will observe the Muslim holidays, express themselves in Muslim terminology and act like Muslims. Do not expect to see crosses in their homes any more than you would expect to see one in a Jewish Messianic home. We have to correct our thinking and expectation that a Muslim background believer automatically becomes a cultural Christian when he or she receives Jesus as personal savior from their sins. This certainly will not happen in the Middle East where a vast majority of the people are Muslims and have as much as 1400 years of tradition as Muslims. Jesus is entering the Muslim world from within and beginning to transform Muslims individually, as groups and hopefully as nations as the Holy Spirit enlightens their hearts through the reading and hearing of the Word of God in the Bible and through the testimony of other Muslim background believers and Christian friends. If you expect a Muslim background believer to automatically become a "Christian" you will be disappointed in this book. But if you are willing to let God work from within the Muslim community as he did in the Jewish and Gentile community in the first century and is still working today, then you may benefit, and your Muslims friends in turn.

I am grateful to my friends "Hamdi," "Barnabas," "Fredrick Wedge," "Ferruchi," "Athanasios" and many others who have taught me, increased my patience and led me to trust the Lord more in my life's calling. I also owe my prayer life to a Muslim I only met once, "Trusty Hajj" who inspired me to practice daily prayer and Bible study through his prayer rug in the YMCA at the University of Virginia in 1953. Many expatriate friends whom I cannot number have inspired, informed and corrected me through the years as I have tried to assist Muslim friends in drawing closer to Jesus. My wife, who is a lovely Rose, has patiently and wisely shared her gift of discernment in encouraging me. To all and especially to the Lord, I am grateful, and dedicate the following

Endnotes: Introduction

[1] Ray G. Register, Jr., *Dialogue and Interfaith Witness with Muslims*, ISBN 978-0-9796019-3-4; GlobalEdAdvancePress, 2007 (IAM Partners, PO Box 463045, Escondido, CA 92046-3045)

[2] Fran Love & Jeleta Eckheart, Editors, Ministry to Muslim Women, *Longing to Call Them Sisters,* William Carey Library, 2000.

[3] William Baker, *Arabs, Islam, and the Middle East,* 2003

[4] Roy Oksnevad, *Leadership Development Within the Muslim Background Believer Community,* Unpublished paper for DME 914 Leadership Development and Culture, May 22-June 2, 2006.

CHAPTER 1

THEIR RELIGIOUS AND CULTURAL BACKGROUND

Muslims are unique people and distinct from cultural Christians in many ways. In order to help Muslim background believers grow in their knowledge of Christ we must recognize where they are different as well as how they are similar to Christians. Again, I am most acquainted with Palestinian Muslims from the Holy Land, but will try to share some ways that Muslims in general differ from the average Christian to enable you to adapt the Gospel to their unique ways of thought and life style.

The basic motive of the Muslim religion, from which Muslim background believers in Jesus come, is the fear of God (Arabic: *takwah*). God is feared, because according to the Quran, the Muslim's Holy Book, God is a righteous judge who will bring every man to judgment on the Last Day.[1] The motive force of Islam is the fear of Hell fire. The mournful call to prayer from the Mosque five times a day strikes fear into the hearts of the followers of Muhammad. I once asked a Muslim background believer why the call to prayer from the Mosque sounded so awesome and he told me it was because Islam is a religion of force and fear. There is a spirit that permeates the reading of the Quran and the prayers of Muslims that captivates the hearts of Muslims. The shout, "Allahu Akbar" (Arabic: God is greater) is a battle cry used to send fear into the hearts of the enemies of Islam, and to give courage to Muslim fighters and suicide bombers. It is also the "hinge of prayer" which the Muslim chants every time they bow in daily prayers. When you disciple a Muslim background believer you need to recruit numerous prayer partners to pray for you and your Muslim friend for protection and freedom from the power of fear that once dominated the Muslim's life. Fear not only dominates the religion of Islam, it acts as a deterrent for Muslims leaving Islam. An apostate, or *murtad*, who leaves Islam for Christianity, is under the threat of death.

The fear motive of Islam stands in stark contrast to the love motive of Christianity. As John Ashcroft is reputed to have said, "Islam is a religion whose God demands you to give your son as a sacrifice for him. Christianity is a religion whose God gives his son as a sacrifice for you!" The selfless "agape" love of the Christian Gospel is unknown in Islam. The God of Islam would never have a son, and if he did, he would certainly not give him as a sacrifice for man, who is regarded as a slave of God. We must be aware of the two major objections of the Muslim religion to the Gospel when discipling Muslim background believers. First, Islam rejects the Sonship and divinity of Jesus Christ, and secondly it rejects his sacrificial death on the cross. There are special ways that these two major doctrines can be explained to a Muslim background believer which we will clarify later. The claim that "Islam is a religion of peace and love," is a recent innovation adapted for Western consumption by Sufi proponents. It has little truth in reality.

Along with the fear motive in Islam, the capriciousness of God in Islam also affects the Muslim background believer's attitude toward the Gospel and toward truth in general. According to the Quran, God can change his mind. The Quran is a collection of piecemeal sayings that Muhammad claims to have received from God on various occasions during his prophetic lifetime. God would often give to Muhammad a better verse than he gave before which substitutes for the former verse as the situation demanded. An entire system of abrogation was created by Muslim scholars to determine which verse was revealed last and is therefore more authoritative. In the Christian-Muslim polemic the Muslim will often tell the Christian, "Your Scripture has been changed," or, "The Quran is the last Word from God." This is a carry over from the theory of abrogation in the Quran. It also affects the Muslim attitude toward history, and makes it very difficult for a Muslim to have a regard for any history prior to Muhammad who lived in the 7-8th Century AD. In his opinion, Islam was revealed last, and therefore supersedes both Judaism and Christianity. According to the Quran, "the religion of God is Islam."[2]

The combination of the capriciousness of God and the fear motive that dominates Islam leads Muslim background believers to exhibit a great degree of distrust in personal relationships. I knew a husband and wife who did not know the other was a believer in Jesus until about six months in the faith. They both showed up at the same meeting and were surprised to see each other! Distrust is an ingrained feature in people from Islamic background. There is a verse in the Quran that says that "God is the greatest of deceivers!"[3] Maintaining a climate of confidentiality is necessary to generate trust with Muslim background believers. We must realize that they could pay with their lives if betrayed.

Distrust is also engendered by the practice of not having always to tell the truth in Muslim society. What is considered as deception and outright lying is unfortunately a matter of lifestyle in some Muslim cultures. The truth can be twisted according to what a Muslim thinks the listener wants to hear. Everyone assumes that there is an ulterior motive behind what is being said. It is customary for a Muslim to be allowed to lie in at least three circumstances. First, a man can tell each wife he loves her best in order to keep harmony in the home. Secondly, he can tell a lie to deceive an enemy of Islam in time of war. And thirdly, he can tell a lie to convert a person to Islam. These lies are all justified as a means to a good end. You can expect a Muslim background believer to tell you many times the story behind the story as to why he or she could not tell the blunt truth in a given situation.

Fatalism is also dominant in Islam and leads to an attitude of resignation to whatever life brings. "Insha Allah," (if God wills) is the answer to most questions about a Muslim's plans for the future. While this certainly has some positive aspects in the complexities of today's world, it can be a cop out from assuming responsibility for one's actions. A Muslim background believer's willingness to admit a mistake or wrongdoing is an indication that the Gospel is beginning to affect their life. Jesus says in John 8:32, "You shall know the truth and the truth shall set you free." A Muslim never knows for certain that he will go to heaven. Muslim suicide bombers are deceived into believing that martyrdom insures a place in Paradise. Contrary to the Quran they are taught that to destroy others and themselves is a way to atone for their sins. What a difference when a Muslim understands the salvation in Jesus Christ. The wife of my friend Barnabas, "Lydia," said that when she accepted Christ, she felt like a new born babe. She knew she had been set free from the guilt of sin. Discipling Muslim background believers demands a careful balance between the need to live a righteous life and at the same time to rely on the grace of God to continually cleanse us from all sin.

History has not been kind to the Muslim countries from which most Muslim background believers come. Many have a love-hate relationship with the west. They abhor what they consider the sexual looseness of Westerners, but at the same time they covet the freedom to act as they please. They have a deep anger over the victories of Israel over the Muslim dominated Middle East. Christine Mallouhi amplified the reasons for this anger in her description of "The Problem of Palestine" in her thoughtful book, *Waging Peace on Islam*.[4] Privately I have heard Palestinians express an admiration for what the Jews have done in that tiny country. They know that their own leaders have squandered the wealth that God has given them through the rich oil fields. The Palestinians, while fiercely loyal to the dream of a state of their own, are very disillusioned by the inability of their leaders to bring them to this goal. I am amazed at the change that comes into the life of a Muslim background believer when he or she studies the Bible and sees the plan that God has for both the Arabs and the Jews. One proof of a real born-again experience is when a Muslim loses their hatred for the Jewish people and vise versa.

You must also be aware of the Muslim's attitude toward sex when discipling or counseling Muslim background believers. Muslims have a very earthy attitude toward sex. Marriage for a Muslim is made on earth, not in heaven. It is a legal contract between a man and a woman (or up to four women!) which provides for the care of each wife and her children in return for her exclusive sexual favors given only to her husband. The Arabic expression a man uses for his wife in the Muslim community is *"hurmi"* that is; the one that is permitted for me and forbidden to others. The popular word for the *haram* comes from the Arabic word meaning to forbid. A Muslim background believer who is new in the faith can easily propose marriage to a single woman who may be divorced or a widow, even though he already has other wives. We had to explain to Muslim background believers that this was simply not done in the Christian community. Some Muslim background believers who come to Christ already have multiple wives. It is interesting to watch the dynamics as God deals with this situation. In the two cases I dealt with personally, the men eventually gave each wife and her children a home and part of the property and lived with the youngest wife. They did not divorce the older wives since this would have disgraced the wives in their Muslim community. The Gospel spread through multiple family groups as each wife came to the Lord.

The attitude of the Muslim is that Islam builds a fence around women to protect them. They assume the woman is the weaker vessel, and is unable to control her desires. In any case, where a woman commits fornication or adultery, she is assumed to be the guilty party. "She gave me a face", similar to the western expression, "She gave me the eye," is the justification for a man to make advances to a woman. In Middle Eastern society a woman who goes astray sexually is killed by her family. Muslim women live in daily fear that their husband will divorce them or bring in a second, third or fourth wife. She is legally prohibited from objecting since a woman cannot testify by herself against a man in a Muslim court. According to the Quran, it takes two women to testify against a man, since a woman is only worth one half of a man legally. The deep fears that women live with in the Muslim world gives a divine opportunity for a Christian woman to encourage Muslim women. I have known Christian women who have experienced the trauma of divorce who have had great opportunities to disciple Muslim woman because there is an immediate affinity with each other's suffering. It is always wise for a woman to be chaperoned when in the company of a Muslim man, so as not to give occasion to the flesh. Anytime a man is alone with a woman who is not his wife, mother or sisters, or close female relative, others in the Muslim community assume it is for a sexual liaison.

Miriam Adeney described graphically the disadvantage women face in Islam. "In Islam, women are polluted and polluting. All bodily processes that secret substances are unclean. Men must wash ceremonially after urinating, defecating, ejaculating semen, or touching something ritually unclean. Women do more: They menstruate, give birth, suckle infants, and clean up children's messes. Menstruating women cannot pray. God will not hear them. Pregnant and nursing women do not fast. Given a high birth rate, a woman may miss fasts for years. But every missed prayer and fast adds to a person's spiritual indebtedness. All in all, then women are always "behind" spiritually. And "this required abstention from worship is a proof of their deficiency in faith," according to a saying attributed to the prophet Muhammad. Even though women may try to "make up" days of prayer and days of fasting, they never really catch up with what God requires.[5]

While we are thinking about the special situation of discipling Muslim women it is good to understand the prevalence of folk Islam among women. Muslim women are very dependant on occult practices to gain power in a male dominated society. The use of incantations, potions, amulets, prayers to saints, and various other forms of occult practice are prevalent in Muslim society, especially among women. It is common for Muslim women to read tea leaves or coffee grounds in a cup to determine the future. Miriam Adeney affirms, "As for religion, many Muslim women know little about Islamic doctrine and theology. They resort to folk religion, shrines, sacrifices, amulets, divination, and spirit possession as often as they turn to Muslim institutions."[6] Other resources for a better understanding of the Muslim reliance on the occult is Bill Musk's book, *The Unseen Faces of Islam,* and *Muslims, Majic and the Kingdom of God* by Rick Love.[7]

Many Muslim women consult sheiks or occult practitioners for health and marriage problems. The use of magical words is very common. The "bismallah" or blessing "in the name of God" is uttered many times during the day and even at the moment of the conception of a child, so that every act comes under the protection of Allah. *Halal* or permitted food is from those animals slaughtered in the name of Allah.

The ideal man, according to Islam, follows the practices or *Sunnah* of the Prophet Muhammad. The way he dresses, talks, eats, drinks, does business, sleeps, goes to the toilet and has sex is supposed to mimic the practices of Muhammad. Muslims pride themselves that Muhammad had the strength to sleep with all of his dozen wives on the same night! Western Christian women who attempt to disciple their Muslim background believer friends should be aware that Muslim women dress modestly as a measure not to cause undue excitement on the part of the men in their company. Also do not be surprised that a male child is looked upon with much more favor in the Muslim home than a girl. The leveling of the sexes and uplifting of the role of women in society is a hallmark of the Christian world, though Muslim propagandists would claim otherwise.

A final observation to help you understand the background of Muslim background believers is that many Muslims and in particular, Muslim women, are functionally illiterate. Many women in Muslim countries have not been given the opportunity of an education. Extensive interviews with Mbbs from a number of countries revealed that a vast majority were literate and male in an environment where most are illiterate. Consequently the vast majority of the illiterate and virtually all females get few chances to hear and believe in Muslim lands.[8] Most Muslims come from oral communication societies and respond much better to story telling than to analytical explanations of the Gospel. One mission society which specialized in written material for the Muslim world hired a secular marketing firm to test audience response to their books. They were surprised to find that the majority of the population of the Muslim world especially in the Middle East, are functionally illiterate. They wisely added audio and visual presentations of the Gospel to their materials. You will find that many Muslims who have immigrated to English speaking countries of the world will respond with appreciation to English as a second language (ESL) training.

These are only a few of the characteristics of the backgrounds of many Muslim background believers that I know. Again, I apologize for any stereotypes. You will meet

Muslims who are highly educated, especially in the college and university world and in the business world who will belie these stereotypes. I do not mean to belittle their achievements. They must be recruited and discipled to improve the lot of other Muslims. I truly believe that only faith in the living Christ will restore the image of God in Muslims worldwide and enable them to fulfill the purpose for which God has destined their great nation of people.

Endnotes: Chapter 1

[1] Daud Rahbar, *God of Justice,* Brill, 1960.

[2] Quran 3:19

[3] Quran 3:54

[4] Christine A. Mallouchi, *Waging Peace on Islam,* Monarch Books, 2000, pp. 100-151.

[5] Miriam Adeney, "Why Muslim Women Come to Christ," Ministry to Muslim Women, *Longing to Call Them Sisters,* p. 113, excerpted from her book, *Hagar's Daughters:Ministry with Muslim Women*

[6] Adeney, op.cit. p. 102

[7] Bill A. Musk, *The Unseen Face of Islam,* MARC, 1989, and Rick Love, *Muslims, Magic and the Kingdom of God,* William Carey Library, 2000

CHAPTER 2

HOW DO THEY COME TO THE LORD?

Muslim background believers come to Jesus in many of the same ways that other people come to the Lord. At the same time, they are unique people with special needs and God uses unusual ways to speak to them about Jesus. In recent years I have known many Muslims who came to the Lord through a simple presentation of the Gospel, such as the Four Spiritual Laws adapted especially for Muslims. A multiplicity of approaches and responses are bringing more and more Muslims into the kingdom.

A majority of Muslims come to the Lord through the personal witness of other Muslim family members and friends who have come to know Jesus as savior. Some are led to the Lord through the witness of missionaries, teachers, doctors, nurses, and other Christians. Some come to the Lord through the reading of Scriptures. Others receive Jesus through the radio, television, audio and video cassette presentations of the Gospel, especially the Jesus Film.

You will hear of Muslims receiving Christ through personal visitations of the Lord in dreams and visions. They seem to be particularly sensitive to this type of revelation of the Lord. Some have accepted Christ through physical healings of themselves or loved ones. Others may experience Christ through the casting out of demons.

A common factor seems to be the yearning for a faithful friend who sticks closer than a brother. They find this friend in Jesus, and in the ones who witness to Him. Muslims have many problems and need a friend and advisor whom they can trust. The emptiness of Islamic rituals and the spirit of distrust and murder which pervades many Islamic communities make them hungry for a Word from God.

The Fuller Theological Seminary of World Mission made a survey of Muslim background believers from 39 countries and over 50 ethnic groups and found similar reasons that Muslims come to believe in Jesus.[?][1] Among the reasons given were:

A sure salvation

Muslims are attracted to Jesus because he offers the assurance of salvation. This is contrary to the uncertainty Muslims have regarding their eternal security. I had many Muslim friends tell me about the thread that they believed is stretched over Hell Fires that all Muslims must pass over on the Day of Judgment. If their bad deeds outweighed their good deeds they would fall into the fire. The assurance of the forgiveness of their sins by Jesus is a major reason they come to accept him as personal savior.

Jesus

The pure and sinless nature of Jesus is a major attraction to Muslim background believers. The willingness to forgive even those who crucified him is totally opposite from the Muslim motivation for retaliation. The Muslim knows in his heart that Muhammad had to pray for the forgiveness of his sins. Only Jesus was sinless. Attempts of Muslim apologists to instill the belief of the sinlessness of all the prophets, including Muhammad, are a weak copy of the nature of Jesus Christ.

The Bible

Muslims are attracted to God in Christ though the testimony of the Bible. The Quran has a high view of the Bible as Holy Scripture, which belies the common belief among Muslims that the Bible has been corrupted. As I found while discipling Barnabas, the Fuller survey found that the Sermon on the Mount is the section of Scripture most helpful to the new Muslim background believer. Genesis, Psalms and Proverbs are also very much liked by new Muslim background believers, along with the Gospel of John. The Book of Acts serves as a guidebook for church planting movements. Muslims find that the Bible contains the truth that amplifies and corrects the Bible stories that the Quran tells in sometimes vague ways. The Bible clarifies the context of God' Words to man.

Dreams and visions

The Fuller survey revealed that a quarter or 25% of new Muslim background believers credited dreams and visions as a vital part of their conversion experience. My friends Muhammad and Barnabas and others related many times about dreams and visions they had which gave them guidance and encouragement in their spiritual growth and trials. Similar to the Fuller survey they often related to seeing the Lord dressed in white as He came to give them courage in difficult situations in life. Muhammad had a dream of his father who had recently died, telling him to listen to the missionaries because they have the truth.

Dreams and visions should be treated cautiously. One Muslim background believer I knew told his parents that he had a vision of Jesus which justified his becoming a Christian and being baptized. He later confessed to me that he had invented this story to justify his conversion. He did not think his parents would be persuaded if he told them the truth that he had grown up in a Christian school and this positive experience had led him to become a Christian. Despite the occasional invention of stories, dreams and visions are known worldwide to play a significant part in convincing Muslims to turn to Christ.

Love

The Fuller survey found that the most compelling reason for the greatest number of Muslims turning to Christ was the power of love. This included the love they saw between Christian believers, as well as the love of God they experienced when they became convinced of Jesus' sacrifice for their sins. They saw in God's love in Jesus a contrast to the love in Islam and the Quran which was a partial love. One Muslim background believer remarked sadly that Islam was "a tool used by Arabs to oppress non-Arabs."[2]

Relationship with God

Some 10% of the Muslim background believers in the Fuller survey related that a relationship with God as friend and father was a factor in their accepting Christ. One of the main reasons a Muslim with multiple wives can adapt to a monogamous life style is the teaching of Christ's love for the church as the bride of Christ in the Epistles. God in Christ offers a personal relationship to the Muslim background believer that cannot be found in Islamic teaching. It is highly possible that the opening verses of the Quran, "In the name of God, the compassionate, the merciful," is a disguised adaptation of the Trinitarian expression, in the name of the Father, Son, and Holy Spirit. There is a relationship of love in the Godhead which is felt by the Muslim background believer.

Blessing in persecution

The Fuller survey found, as we found among Palestinian Muslim background believers, that persecution played a great role in strengthening the faith of new believers. The Muslim background believers I have known suffered beatings, burnings, accidents, divorce, poverty, illness, and starvation. But despite it all, most remained steadfast and even grew in their faith. I once asked the Lord why the believers had to suffer so much and it was as if he told me, "I am molding them into my image." The verse in Mathew 5:11 in the Sermon on the Mount which says, "Blessed are you when they revile you and persecute you, and say all kinds of evil against you falsely for my sake," is certainly a reality for most the Muslim background believers I have known.

Another study presented in a conference in Canada listed the following paths that lead to Christ:[?][3]

1.   Read Gospel Story.
2.   See Jesus in dream or vision.
3.   Struggle with evil spirits—find name of Jesus frees them.
4.   Abused or in dysfunctional relationship—greater power in Jesus.
5.   Long for justice in society and find this in Jesus.
6.   Desperate for freedom from immoral lifestyle.
7.   Fearing death and longing for assurance of paradise.
8.   Women find that Jesus affirms them.
9.   Since a child, longed for intimacy with God and finds it in Jesus.

Miryam Edeney expanded on five milestones that recur in Muslim women coming to Christ: Scripture, power encounters, the love of Christians, sex and beauty issues and social justice issues in "Ministry to Muslim Women." She explains, "God, whom the Muslims call, "the merciful and compassionate," demonstrates those qualities of mercy and compassion most of all in Christ. This is why Muslim women come to Christ. Through Christ, the God who they knew incompletely and from afar becomes their heavenly Father."[4]

Ulterior Motives

Those who disciple Muslims must be aware of the many motivations which cause them to become inquirers. These motivations are so dominant that many Eastern Christians distrust Muslims who claim to be believers. We must admit that some of us come to Christ with ulterior motives. We therefore do not judge the Muslim who seeks him, but we must not be naïve.

Some Muslims will expect to receive a Christian wife when they accept Christ. Muslim wives will sometimes refuse to sleep with their believing husbands as a way to force them to return to Islam. Often the families of the wives will pressure them into refusing to sleep with their believing husbands. I knew a Palestinian government official who became a believer. His wife, under pressure from an elder aunt who lived with them, refused to sleep with him. After several months of a celibate life he came to me and told me the problem. He said, "I cannot live like this. You have to get me a Christian wife!" I asked him how long it took for him to receive the Lord? He told me, "Several years." I then suggested he be patient with his wife, especially since it took him so long to come to Christ and he knew she was being pressured by her family. He waited and she soon reconciled with him.

There have been occasions in the Churches in the Middle East where a Muslim has come into the fellowship pretending to be a believer. Unfortunately, when he marries a Christian girl and leaves the fellowship, it is devastating to the dwindling Christian community. Christian girls and women are forced into marriages in some countries, only deepening the mistrust against Muslims who claim to be believers in Jesus. That is a major reason for encouraging Muslim background believers to marry women from their own community, if these women will tolerate, or better still, adopt the faith of their husbands. If we insist that Muslims become "cultural Christians" we will be expected to provide them with a new family and possibly a new wife.

Another ulterior motive some Muslims come to the Lord with is the expectation of financial help. Muslims are usually in great financial need, especially if they have multiple wives and numerous children. I once knew a Muslim teacher who came to us as a new believer. He had three wives and numerous children. He was a man with great potential and influence. I helped him buy a used computer for his high school aged son. Unfortunately, he decided instead to order a much more expensive Pentium computer while I was out of the country and used my name as a guarantee. He had his wife sign a check for this more expensive computer. The check bounced. When I returned to the country the computer store manager told me that I owed him for the computer! I told him I had been out of the country and showed him my passport and visa stamp as proof. He called the man and told him that the check had been returned and he was going to report his wife to the police if he did not make it good. The only alternative was to return the Pentium to me and take the other computer that I had ordered for him. The man said he would comply. When I arrived at his house with another believer I changed the computers. The teacher arrived before we left and began cursing me since I had discovered his deception. This man left our fellowship and tried to turn other Muslim background believers against us. He did not succeed. He tried to get the police to investigate other believers. He persisted in making problems and threats for the believers until one day he dropped dead on the street.

Another man we will call "Sam" claimed to receive the Lord as a result of meeting believers in the taxi he drove. He was taken in and interrogated by the Secret Police and imprisoned for almost a month. Due to pressure from expatriate believers he was finally released after being threatened by the police. He fled the country with his wife and six children. We assisted Sam to live at our conference center for almost a year. He had Bible studies in his home and many of his relatives joined the Muslim believer's movement because of him. On one occasion I mentioned his case to a leading politician from his home country. This man told me that our friend was deceiving us. I had some doubts about Sam. He had a secret life which caused conflict with his wife. I felt that his wife and children were sincere. Due to political problems he was never able to get a work permit in our country. Sam was in desperate financial straits and I helped to raise a sum of money to pay his house rent, even over the objections of some of my ministry partners. I made the first admitted mistake of my career. I gave Sam the money rather than giving it to his landlord. Early the next morning he fled back to his home town, leaving all his Bibles and tracts in the empty apartment. His landlord dumped them in the trash. Sam took the money I had given him and finished his house in his home town. The upshot of the story is, Sam was jailed again, tortured and was struck dumb. His girlfriend from his home town was shot and killed. Evidently they had been running a prostitution ring. Sam had refused to let his own daughters get involved. He eventually died in prison.

These are sad stories which reveal that Muslims come to the Lord with many motivations and problems. But there can be a silver lining. One Muslim background believer categorizes "converts" into the following types:

1.   Grateful Converts: They feel Christ set them free and they are very grateful to him.
2.   Switching Converts: They feel that Islam is not fulfilling and they are attracted to the West so they adopt the western faith.
3.   Hating converts: Mostly they hate Islam for a personal reason, they are believers in God and they could not live without believing in something.
4.   Converts with expectations: Those who think that they will gain some benefits by their conversion.

It is because Muslim background believers come to the Lord with many and various motivations and baggage that they are your best mentors and coaches in work with other Muslims. They already know what is in their minds and hearts. They will warn you about deception and possible danger. They will give you feedback after visits with other Muslims and tell you who was really interested in the Gospel. They will coach you on words and methods to use in witnessing and discipling other Muslims. It is only a short step to releasing them to be the frontline person to lead other Muslims into the Kingdom and to disciple them into mature believers.

We must not omit the most powerful reason Muslims are coming to Christ in unprecedented numbers today; the power of prayer. Since the "10/40 Window" emphasis in prayer was started about the time of the first Gulf War in the early 1990's Muslims have started turning to Christ. Christians in the West finally awoke to the fact that if they do not pray for Muslims the Muslims will be their eternal enemy. It took the shock of the battle field to arouse the attention of the Christian world to the need of Muslims for a personal relationship with God through faith in Jesus as Savior and Lord. The attacks on the USA on 9/11 drove home the desperate need of praying for Muslims to come to Christ before they turn themselves into suicide bombers. We now have an Email network of over 700 people praying for one specific Muslim unreached people group and there are many more networks for prayer. God is remaining faithful to answer these prayers and to send forth laborers into the harvest. Many are paying the ultimate price for witnessing and discipling Muslims in this harvest.

Now that we understand a little better the motives of Muslims who come to us, or whom the Lord allows us to influence for him, we need to look at our attitudes as disciplers and mentors of Muslim background believers.

Endnotes: Chapter 2

[1] J. Dudley Woodberry and Russell G. Shubin, "*Why I chose Jesus*", http://www./missionfrontier.org/2001/01/muslim.htm

[2] ibid. p. 10

[3] "Many Paths Lead to Christ, VMMP Conference, Burnaby, BC, Canada-1 November 2003, copied from G. Stevenson, "Meeting the Needs of Mbbs in North America, COMMA Conference, Wheaton, IL, 2003

[4] Miriam Adeney, Ministry to Muslim Women, p. 103

CHAPTER 3

ATTITUDES NEEDED
BY COUNSELORS AND MENTORS
OF MUSLIM BACKGROUND BELIEVERS

An attitude of acceptance is essential in discipling Muslim background believers. We need to accept the Muslims for who they are and the Gospel for the power it has to change their lives. How are you going to react when a Muslim comes to you to be discipled and he has two or three wives? Do you feel it is more necessary to change his lifestyle and that of his wives than it is to teach him the essentials of the Gospel message? Do you trust the power of the Gospel to change his or her heart and in the process to change their lifestyle? Paul declared, "For I am not ashamed of the gospel, for it is the power of God for salvation to everyone who believes,,, for in it the righteousness of God is revealed from faith to faith."[1] In other words, the Gospel has the power of God to save and then to lead to right living when a Muslim receives it in faith.

Dealing with the matter of polygamy is a challenge for those of us from Christian monogamous backgrounds. It can have its interesting moments. A sister of my friend Hamdi was married to a man who decided to marry another wife. At first she was upset and went home to her brother. We prayed for her. She later decided to return home since her husband gave her the honored position in the family. She became the mentor for the younger wife. Later the family visited in our home. My wife and I noticed with amusement as the two wives swapped positions next to the husband at our dinner table and serving in the kitchen! The children of the older wife became high achievers. Through our acceptance of this situation we were able to share the Gospel with the families involved on numerous occasions.

Muslim background believers see our example in our monogamous married life and this becomes a model for them in the discipling process. We are able to share with them the secret of the monogamous love of a husband for his wife, that is, Christ's love for the Church. At the same time, we must be careful that we do not get infected by the spirit of polygamy in Islam. I know of at least two colleagues working with Arabs who divorced their wives and married other women, bringing untold sadness to their wives and families.

We also need an intense loyalty to the Bible as the written Word of God, while at the same time an acceptance of the use of the Quran as a bridge to dialogue and witness. If you attack Muhammad and the Quran you will most likely offend the Muslim so much that it could drive them back further into Islam. My own parents had some glowing weaknesses, but I did not like anyone outside my immediate family talking about them! Criticism of Muhammad and the Quran is usually counter productive in both witness and discipling Muslim background believers. It is better to allow the Muslim background believer to make their own comparison of Muhammad and Jesus. I never challenge a Muslim to do this. This is usually an exercise the Christian Arabs like to do. I prefer to assign Christian Arabs the exercise of comparing Muhammad to Peter or Moses, since I do not believe there is any equal to Jesus, either in the Bible or in the Quran. The Quran elevates Jesus above all the prophets. The honest Muslim will already realize this. Jesus, according to the Quran, is born of a virgin, is a Word and Spirit from God, creates life, heals the sick, raises the dead, suffers rejection, dies, is closest to God , and is returning again. Therefore, properly explained and amplified by the Bible, the

Quran can become a bridge for faith in Jesus.

Muslims are very sensitive to our attitude toward them. Before I would bring untested persons with me on visits to Muslims I would invite them to my home at a time my friend Hamdi would be there. I would leave them alone with him for a few minutes. Later he would tell me whether the person loved Muslims or not. One well known Christian Arab evangelist visited his town and spoke out against a prominent Muslim clergyman. I was told never to bring him back again.

Trust is an essential element in discipling Muslim background believers. They must be able to trust us. We may be the only friend they can really trust. Therefore, we should never give their names to other people, especially other Muslims, without their permission. We should not brag about Muslim background believers, nor write their names in publications without their permission. We should let them do their own testifying. Remember, they could lose their jobs, families and lives if the wrong person were to learn about them.

Friendship and loyalty are essential attitudes in dealing with Muslim background believers. You will have a hard time winning a hearing or doing effective discipling and mentoring if you offend the Muslim background believer. Saving face, or "whitening the face" (Arabic: beyadh al-wiji) is important in Muslim and Eastern cultures. The positive reward of friendship with Muslims is that you will be remembered as long as they live.

Speaking the truth in love, or honesty, is also a needed characteristic or attitude in discipling and mentoring Muslim background believers. Remember, they live in a world full of half truth and deceit. They naturally look for the motive behind every act and word. You must be as wise as a serpent and as harmless as a dove. The Muslim background believer will sometimes tell you what they think you want to hear rather than the whole truth behind a matter. We must remember that they are under the threat of a *murtad,* or apostate, by fanatical Muslims and could loose their lives it they are betrayed in a situation in which they do not have protection or security.

The attitude of the mentor or discipler of Muslim background believers is very important in discipling them. Much wisdom and patience is needed. There are methods that will enhance the process of spiritual growth which will be presented in the next chapter.

Endnote: Chapter 3

[1] 1 Romans 1:16

CHAPTER 4

METHODS OF DISCIPLING

The two New Testament keys of discipling Muslim background believers are to find the "man (and woman!) of peace and to disciple them on condition that they disciple other Muslims.[1] Jesus practiced and mentored this method as he trained and sent his disciples out two by two to preach the Gospel. He selected key men, trained and discipled them and sent them out to share all that they learned. He empowered them for their task and gave them his blessing as they went forth. He carried out his ministry in their own towns so they could see how he did it, and then reap the harvest behind him. When they had practiced he sent them forth in pairs to cast out demons and to heal every disease and infirmity.[2] They returned rejoicing when God blessed them with a harvest. We will see the same results when we seek out those Muslims God has called to salvation, teach them and send them back to their own people, trusting the Word of God and the Spirit of God to empower them for the harvest.

The first method of discipling Muslim background believers is to make a contract or covenant with them; that what you teach them, and model for them, they will in turn teach others. As Paul told Timothy, "what you have heard from me before many witnesses entrust to faithful men who will be able to teach others also."[3] If we wait until we think a Muslim has understood everything, or become as mature as we think they should be, in order to empower them to tell others, we will never see a church planting movement among them. It was when I trusted the Lord and the power of his Word and Spirit to empower Muslims to teach others that I began to see the harvest I had prayed for years to see.

I mentioned earlier about Sam who betrayed me and went back to his hometown with the rent money. Before he left, his friend who I call Barnabas, sneaked my mobile phone number off Sam's phone when Sam went to the bathroom. He called me and told me he had to see me. He told me that he had been married to a Christian wife some years back in another country. She had taken him to the Orthodox Church, but he could not understand their prayers. He wanted me to teach him how to become a Christian, how to live with his wives (!) as a Christian, how to raise his children as Christians, how to pray, fast and worship as a Christian. I agreed on one condition; that what I taught him he would pass on to others. He agreed. I led him through the Four Spiritual Laws and he received Christ. He later called me and told me he met a friend who wanted to hear the "Four." I told him, "On one condition; Next time you give him the Four!" We met for Bible study and prayer almost daily for several weeks until he was baptized. Later he called me and told me that some young men in the Arab villages had received the Four and wanted to be baptized. He feared that if I baptized them that they would be interrogated by the secret police. So, I told him, "You baptize them! Do it the way I baptized you. If you need any help call me and I will coach you by mobile phone." He began to disciple and baptize other Muslim background believers. The church planting movement started to grow.

When it became known in his family that he was a believer in Jesus each wife began to react differently. He was married to three women, each living in a separate city. The oldest wife was sickly, having borne him eight children. She nearly died giving birth to the last son. They were about to send her to a hospital in another country to die. So, we prayed for her. She got well! The result was that she and all her adult children scattered throughout the area became believers, and the movement grew more.

His middle wife was a fundamentalist Muslim. She divorced him and demanded the *nafaka*, or alimony. She opened a case against him in the local Muslim *Shariah* Court. He had to scramble around to come up with the money to settle with her. Her oldest daughter, a very bright high school student became a believer in Jesus. She began to discover teachers in her school who were secret believers, so the movement grew even more.

His third wife, the youngest, held out the longest. Her brother was a *sheikh* and she feared his reaction. When she finally came through for the Lord, he beat her up and kicked her out of the family home. His two oldest sons became believers, as well as his brother. His mother was a silent supporter of the Muslim believer's movement until her death. It seems that she had taken her family to a Catholic Church when they live in a Christian village. Barnabas' youngest wife, who we now call "Lydia" attended a Quaker High School and spoke some English. She became a Bible woman and witnessed to many of her family and friends. Her sisters became believers and many of their children accepted the faith. The movement kept growing. One day Barnabas told me it was difficult in the Muslim culture for a man to baptize a woman who was not from his own family. He asked me, "What do you think if Lydia was to baptize the women?" I told him, "I do not think we Baptists do it that way." He responded, "Well, you better get used to it because we do!" The movement began to mushroom. Her nephews and nieces began student movements in the Universities they attended. The student leader in one university became our first martyr when he was stabbed after being accused of being a *kafir*, or apostate, during a student demonstration.

I share this experience to reinforce the method of concentrating on the "man and woman of peace" who in turn will share the Gospel with their friends and relatives, while remaining cultural Muslims. I kept checking to see what they were teaching their friends and family, and coached them in methods of Bible study, discussion, and gave them basic instructions in holding of meetings, the Lord's Supper and baptisms.

The main point to emphasize is; Muslims learn by doing. We cannot expect them to become perfect overnight. The most important method of discipling them is one-on-one Bible study and prayer. We will talk more in the next chapter about the content of these studies.

Muslim believers accommodate themselves readily to small groups. Muslims love to socialize. Each Muslim culture has rituals of entertaining. The Arab Muslim culture is rich in hospitality. They are very group and family oriented. They love to socialize over coffee and food. They are an oral culture. Therefore small groups comprising of friends, family, or affinity groups are a natural method of gathering Muslims for their own lay-led Bible studies and discussion groups.

A middle aged woman studying in a Christian College in Georgia asked me to recommend a project in a Muslim town to her for her mission class. I was able to place her in a woman's club in a town near a major historic Muslim city. She and her teenage children spent their evenings in a local Christian hospice and she worked with the women's club during the day, teaching English as a second language. She made friends with the leader of the woman's club and her daughter. When the summer project was over, she left a Bible in Arabic with the leader of the women's club. The woman had her daughter read the Bible to her and the other women in the club. Soon there was a believers group gathered in the woman's club. Later, the leader suffered kidney failure. Another Muslim background believer, a male who lived in a nearby town, donated a kidney to her. She died about a year later. There were so many Muslim background believers at her funeral that the local sheikhs became angry and left her home. The believers were then able to have a Christian funeral for her, as she had requested before she died.

Muslim background believers meet often for fellowship, eating and prayer. They meet any time, any where and they meet often. They do not necessarily have regular meeting places. We have had meetings in cars, in fields, under trees, in garages, in stores, in homes, and occasionally in churches when these are available and open to having Muslims meet with them. A point to note is, if the meeting becomes too visible it can bring a backlash from fanatical fundamentalist Muslims in the community. One group I knew used to meet in a kindergarten building in the evening. The building was burned at least twice, and the homes of the believers in the area were burned. High visibility of Muslim background believers meetings can be counterproductive in the beginning of a church planting movement due to severe opposition of other less tolerant Muslims.

Muslims will usually adopt the ecclesiology of the one who wins them to the Lord and disciples them. I used to take the Muslim background believers to a number of different churches after explaining to them the different forms of worship of the Baptists, Pentecostals, Episcopals, Catholics, and Messianic Jews. Churches are often scarce in predominantly Muslim countries. In the end, my believers preferred to return to the Baptist meetings because of their quiet simplicity and lack of political emphasis. We never saw a movement among them toward a "Jesus Mosque." Most of the believers in our movement quit praying in the mosque years ago, and would not prefer to go back to that style of prayer. I noticed that if I held my hands out in prayer as Muslims do and prayed with my eyes open, the Muslim believers would do the same. If I did not, they would pray just as I did with my head bowed and eyes closed. Usually Muslim prayer forms were more effective as a bridge to unbelieving Muslims or to new believers. When a Muslim background believer returns to the mosque to pray it is usually a sign that they have succumbed to community or financial pressure to return to Islam.

Muslims who practiced the ritual prayers before becoming believers are familiar with what Paul described in Philippians 4:6, "Be anxious for nothing, but in everything by prayer and supplication with thanksgiving let your requests be made known to God." Prayer and supplication, or in Arabic: salat wa du'ah are two different functions in prayer. For the Muslims and for many Eastern Christians prayer, or salat, is a physical ritual with scheduled kneelings, and specific words of confession. It is preceded by ritual cleansing or ablutions with water. Supplication, or du'ah is a petition for personal needs and is a private form of prayer. When a Muslim comes to faith in Christ as personal savior he or she can become confused by the evangelical Christian practice of extemporaneous prayer. Many Muslim women do not attend the Mosque and may be totally unfamiliar with this type of prayer. They will have to be taught by example of how to pray from the heart to God as heavenly Father. Also they can be encouraged to "wash their hearts" through the reading or singing of God's word in Scripture which is a spiritual form of ablution referred to in Ephesians 5:26. This kind of personal, intimate communion with God is the secret of spiritual growth for the Muslim background believer, and is reinforced in the corporate group prayer in fellowship groups which become the church. Some churches have written prayer books in Arabic and other local languages of Mbbs which can assist them in verbalizing their prayers. This can be an aid to literate Muslims, but there is no substitute for spontaneous prayer from the heart, which can be expressed by all oral communicators and meet the needs of hungry hearts.

An effective method of discipling Muslim background believers is storying the Gospel. Muslims are oral communicators and are used to memorizing long passages of the Quran by repeating them out loud. They are attracted to the stories in the Bible, beginning in Genesis and ending in Revelation since the core of many of these stories is found in the Quran. Stories have an appeal to all ages. In some areas drama is an effective method of involving Muslim background believers in acting out and testifying to their faith.   A.H., a friend and colleague who teaches Muslim women immigrants the Gospel in the Middle East and Europe explains how we apply the lessons we learn from Jesus and Paul to our situation of discipling MBB women. "First of all, we need to look at the preferred learning style of the women we are discipling. Most Muslim women are oral communicators. Most of the disciples and people around Jesus were oral communicators. Jesus taught them by telling stories, by giving examples, and by modeling for them what to do. The disciples learned in a group and not as individuals. Oral communicators learn in groups and from stories. Jim Bowman, who teaches Chronological Bible Storying, tells us that oral communicators learn by listening, repeating, by example, form a holistic overview and through memorization. They use narrative, oratory, recitation, drama and music. They are event oriented and community oriented." A. H. goes on to explain, "The oral communicator needs a structure into which she can place the truths she is learning. When biblical truth is given in chronological order, she can see how God reveals His truth. Things make sense. She can keep it straight in her mind. Then once she has chronological structure, she can add new stories by putting them into their proper place in the chronological structure. As I would tell you to open your Bible to Genesis 29, I would tell the MBB oral communicator, "You know that Jacob is the Father of Joseph. Today the story tells about Jacob's family." By studying the biblical truths in a group setting, Timothetta can talk about them with her family and friends. As a group, they decide that they can accept and apply the truths learned to their lives. Some would say you couldn't do this sort of study with groups in restricted access countries. Story telling is the natural form of communication and learning for oral communicators. It is possible to tell stories to groups in restricted access areas."[4]

Printed literature, brochures, and correspondence courses are effective discipling tools for Muslims who can read. About 10% of Muslims who take Bible Correspondence courses indicate faith in Christ during the course. The course can be followed by regional seminars for "graduates" that can further solidify and clarify their faith in Christ. It is best that these meetings be held discreetly and at the discretion of the students, due to strong community pressure. I have known those who try to follow up on correspondence students to be very disappointed when they could not find many of the so-called converts. Muslims are much more likely to express their interest in the Gospel in private than to let this interest be known to family and friends who may be hostile to their interest.

One of the most effective correspondence courses in our area was called the Academy of Theological Studies (ATS) led by a Druze background believer for the benefit of Arab Muslims, Druze and Christians. It used newspaper advertisements and word of mouth to recruit students from all levels of the professional society in the Middle East. The ATS enrolled priests and teachers who needed to upgrade their professional credentials to teach religion in the local schools. The program was enhanced by yearly seminars led by professors with academic level degrees. Hundreds of Arabic speaking professionals studied the Bible and at the same time elevated their academic credentials in the community. The only difficulty was that accreditation remained an ongoing problem. Some students were motivated to study simply for the accreditation, but nevertheless heard the Gospel in the process.

The Internet now offers a golden opportunity to disciple Muslim background believers who are computer literate. Such sights as Answering- Islam.org and others offer a wealth of material for the inquiring Muslim background believer, as well as strong apologetic material from the Bible and the Quran. The Muslim believer can study from the privacy of his or her own computer, and can be networked to other believers in their area for mutual support. We must be aware that the Muslim fundamentalist movements are also using the Internet to try to refute the Gospel and entice Christians to become Muslims. Also they watch the Christian Internet sites in order to apprehend inquirers or to sabotage the sites.

Radio and Television, along with audio cassettes and videos play an important role not only in attracting new believers, but also in discipling Muslim background believers. The Gospel Recording Bible storying and church planting audio cassette in Arabic has proven to be an effective tool in discipling Muslim background believers and encouraging them to form believing groups in their local community.[5] The cassettes are available in many languages. One side stories the Gospel message, keyed to a "Wordless Book" and the other side tells about how to witness, disciple believers and form into Bible study groups. We have discovered that using this cassette leads to demands for the Jesus Film which has been one of the best tools of outreach for the Gospel in known history. The Jesus Film is available in many languages and has been adapted recently with a special introduction and closing for Muslims. The recent premier of "The Passion of the Christ" will increase demand for the Jesus Film worldwide and spread the exposure of the Gospel among Muslims.

An area that needs more attention is the production of music for Muslim background believers. Their style of music is much different from that of the west and even that of Arabic Christian believers. Adult Muslim background believers have great difficulty in vocalizing the tunes of the Christian Arabs, though they try! Music is very important in conveying the Gospel message among oral communicators. Music aids in retention of Bible verses and may explain the popularity of the Psalms among Muslim background believers. The Quran has been chanted in the mosque for centuries, copying the chants of the Byzantine Church. For the Middle Eastern mind to recite a verse of scripture is to chant it.

There are many methods of discipling Muslims. The core of all these methods must be the imparting of the Gospel message in the Bible, and the living out of this message in daily life as the Muslim background believer faces the challenges of living their new life with God in an often hostile environment. Those who opposed the disciples in the early Messianic movement noted in Acts 4:13 that "they were unschooled, ordinary men. They were astonished and took note that these men had been with Jesus." What was Jesus' methods in discipling these men who would lead in the building of the church and how can we apply these same methods in discipling Muslim background believers? I note at least these points:

1.   He taught them with authority-We have the same Word, the same Spirit and the same authority.

2.   He lived with them-he had daily contact. Discipling Muslims demand our daily time and togetherness.

3.   He discipled in small groups or 3, 6, or 12. We make a mistake if we look for large numbers. The core men and women of peace need intensive, personal training in order for them to train others.

4.   He knew their capacity to learn. He began simple and only entrusted them with what he could trust them to keep. Security is a major issue for Muslim background believers.

5.   He taught them from the beginning how to deal with opposition and persecution. When you call a Muslim to trust Jesus as Savior and Lord, you call him to come and die!

6.   He disciplined during teachable moments. Peter was a good example, i.e. The confession at Caesarea Philippi, the Lord's Supper, before the cock crowed and even after the resurrection beside the Sea of Galilee. We need to know when to be gentle, firm and direct in discipling Muslim background believers.

In methodology of discipling Muslim background believers it is also important to have times of retreat for them to consider what has been learned and to assess the cost of discipleship. It is better to let the Holy Spirit deal with them rather than to force a premature commitment. We will deal next with the content of discipleship which in some case is unique for Muslim background believers.

Endnotes: Chapter 4

[1] Matthew 10:13, Luke 10:6

[2] Matthew 10:1

[3] 2 Timothy 2:2 RSV

[4] A.H. "Discipleship of MBB Women," unpublished paper and "Discipleship of Muslim Background Believers through Chronological Bible Storying, *Ministry to Muslim Women*, pp. 146-173.

[5] Gospel Recordings, 41823 Enterprise Circle

North, Temecula CA 92590

CHAPTER 5

THE CONTENT OF DISCIPLESHIP

The majority of books written by evangelical Christians about Muslims are geared toward explaining Islam, defending Christianity from the polemical attacks of Muslims and presenting the Gospel to Muslims. They are by and large polemical or apologetic in nature. Now that Muslims are responding in significant numbers to the Gospel around the world, we need to know how to help Muslims grow in their faith in Christ. What is the content, or subject matter of the discipling process? How does it need to be adapted to the particular needs of Muslims who may have little, or at best, distorted information about the Gospel? Recently "The Passion of the Christ" was shown in various Muslim countries. Muslims are viewing the film and asking questions like, "Why is the film different than the Gospels?" "Will you now change the Gospels to fit the film?" Muslims are taught that we have changed the Gospels, and this is a natural reaction for an inquiring Muslim. They are unfamiliar with the differences between a Catholic and an evangelical interpretation of the Gospel story.

We remember from earlier discussion that the Muslim background believer comes to the faith from many and varied motivations and perhaps some misconceptions. They may be sensitive to negative statements about Muhammad and the Quran. They face opposition and open persecution for their willingness and desire to learn more about Jesus and the Bible. It is best to assume, as with any new believer, that the Muslim background believer is starting at zero regarding knowledge of the basics of the Gospel. Perhaps they are hostile to some of the basic principals such as the need for salvation through the shed blood of Jesus on the cross. They are taught from birth that man is not a sinner and no one can die or intercede for another's sins. Despite these learned objections to the Gospel, I have been amazed at the openness of many Muslims to hear the plain message of salvation without argument in the last few years. In the beginning of my ministry to Muslims I hesitated to use the Four Spiritual Laws in witness to them because of their strong objection to the cross. Muslims are taught that Jesus did not die on the cross, but someone else, like Judas Iscariot, was crucified in the place of Jesus. I have heard this argument less and less in recent years. Muslims, whose heart has been opened by the Holy Spirit and their desperate circumstances, are receiving a simple presentation of the Gospel without argument. They may not understand it, but they are not opposing it as was formerly the case.

Therefore, I now recommend the "Four Spiritual Laws" as a basic discipleship tool for Muslim background believers.[1] The basic laws of God's love, his divine plan for your life, our sin which separates us from God, Jesus' death for you and your need to receive this offer of salvation personally are basic to helping the Muslim to understand and experience the new birth. The "Four" are not the last word, but they are a good beginning in the discipleship process. Incidentally, a little brochure, "Sin of Smoking" often provoked inquiries about Jesus, who is given as the answer in this tract to the addiction of smoking that is prevalent in the Middle East.[2] We used to call the Sin of Smoking tract our "hook" and the Four Spiritual Laws our "bait."

My friend Barnabas has created his own 10 steps to discipling Muslim background believers. He feels that the Four Spiritual Laws are too much to absorb by a new believer and are not understood by most Muslim inquirers. Therefore he has steps of discipleship before the Laws and steps after them. He also has special materials designed for leaders of Muslim believers groups.

I found that the Sermon on the Mount contained excellent content for discipling Muslims. It speaks to the desire of the new Muslim background believer to know the basic motivations of the message of Jesus, God's care as a loving heavenly Father, how to pray, fast, treat the poor, deal with family problems and respond to persecution. It gives Jesus' interpretation of key Bible or Old Testament principals of living. The Sermon on the Mount is understood by Muslims, since it is written in Middle Eastern proverbial style and thought form. It was probably used as an early church catechism and is hard to improve on. The Beatitudes make a good study of the stages of personal repentance, acceptance of God's righteousness, purity of heart, peacemaking, and facing persecution for the sake of the kingdom. The Kingdom of Heaven provides for the Muslim background believer a worthy replacement for the Islamic concept of the *ummah*, or the believer's community. The Sermon on the Mount ends with the emphasis of seeking the Kingdom of God and his righteousness. It appeals to the Muslim's desire for worthy motivations for good works, or *niyyat*.

One of the most important aspects of the Sermon on the Mount is the Lord's Prayer, since it gives the Muslim background believer a model for prayer that he or she can use daily to approach God. Christine Mallouchi was asked by Muslim friends, "Do you pray?" They were curious because they had never seen her do the formal kneeling and gestures they are accustomed to calling prayer. She recited for them the Lord's Prayer. The effect of this took her by surprise. "Not only were their spirits touched by its beauty, they were astounded by the implications of 'Forgive as we want to be forgiven' and with one voice they stopped me after that sentence to discuss it. In a culture built on retaliation (Islam along with Judaism believes in an eye for an eye and a tooth for a tooth) free and necessary forgiveness is revolutionary. Since that day I no longer rattle off 'Our Father' but notice how revolutionary the whole prayer is.[3]

My friend Barnabas often struggled with the mixed reception of his family and friends to the Gospel. I was able to remind him that Jesus' parables clarified the type of reaction of various people to the Gospel. The Parable of the Sower or the Soils in Matthew 13:3-23 tells about those whose hearts are harden to the Word but Satan quickly plucks it up. Others receive it with apparent joy, but fall away at the first sign of opposition. Some who receive it do not bear fruit because of their worldly concerns. But, thankfully, there are those who receive the Word, pass it on to others and bear much fruit. Muslims can identify with these word pictures.

The Psalms are a favorite of Muslim background believers who identify with David and others in their struggles to worship God in an often hostile environment. The Psalms offer encouragement when faced with personal failure and persecution. Discipling, counseling and modeling for Muslim background believers is a daily adventure. The Psalms are short enough to provide just the right amount of material for a daily discipling session, which at a minimum, involves sharing, Scripture and prayer. They also contain model prayers that enable the Muslim to express their needs to God.

The Proverbs also provide excellent material for discipling Muslim background believers. New believers of all backgrounds need the wisdom for devotion and living that the Proverbs provide. Muslims are conditioned by their backgrounds to be less than honest in all their dealings with others. The Proverbs are couched in the Middle East mindset regarding one's dealings with peers and with superiors, and appeal to the Muslim who is used to intrigues and deception as a way of life. Proverbs offers down to earth advice in daily living in terms that the Muslim understands.

The Old Testament stories of the Patriarchs provide history and clarifications that benefit the Muslim background believer. The Quran contains brief stories of Adam and Eve, Abraham, Moses, Joseph, Noah, Jonah and other biblical characters. The Book of Genesis is particularly valuable, as well as Exodus. Part of the discipling process is to fill in the blanks and clarify the historical stories of the men and women of old whose lives, sufferings, and prophecies culminate in the coming of salvation in Jesus Christ. Many of the different versions of the stories in the Quran can be attributed to the influence of Jewish folk traditions on Muhammad. Few realize that despite the anti-Jewish rhetoric popular in Islam, the Quran affirms the Promised Land for the Jewish people. Some have attempted to compare Muhammad with the Old Testament prophets due to his judgmental pronouncements on the sins of the Quraish and his multiple marriages. The Muslims, for the most part, finds themselves on familiar territory in the Old Testament. Muslim background believers, when trained in the Old Testament become good witnesses to Jews in showing them the fulfillments of their hopes in Jesus. I have seen Muslims weep when they heard the prophetic words of Isaiah 53, as it speaks of the suffering Messiah.

All of this content of discipling Muslim background believers combined lends itself to the use of storying the Bible for Muslims. Ultimately the Muslim background believer needs to understand the plan of salvation from Genesis to Revelation. Storying the Bible appeals to the Muslim usage of oral tradition and helps to overcome the functional illiteracy that plagues their world. A.H. faces practical issues in discipling Muslim women who have become believers. She explains, "Now that Fatma is a believer, barriers to living a Christ-like life are surfacing. She has practiced Folk Islam all her life. She has always gossiped. She likes to tell off-color stories and jokes. Fatma has 5 children. How will she raise them to know about Jesus? Lies and deceit between husband and wife in her culture are normal. What does she need to know in order to build a Christian marriage and home? Biblical forgiveness doesn't exist in Islam. (Said, 29 March 04) How does Fatma learn to forgive? What should Fatma do with religious holidays like Ramadan and the feasts? Fatma needs to learn how to pray. Her previous experience with prayer doesn't help her now that she is a believer. Fatma and her husband need to get with other believers to form a fellowship that should become a church. What is church? How does she start one? What will happen to Fatma when others learn she is a Christian? She needs to hear Jesus' teachings about persecution. Fatma needs also to learn about end times and how Jesus will come again. Most summers Fatma and her family go back to their country to their original home village for vacation. Fatma needs to learn how to share her stories with her family and friends back in her home country...With Chronological Bible Storying, the evangelism story track is based on the worldview issues that keep Muslim women from accepting Christ as well as the essential biblical truths about living a Christ-like life as well as on the worldview issues that keep Muslim Background Believers (MBB) from developing a mature faith that they can share with others. In preparing stories to share with MBB women like Fatma, I want to know what the issues are with her life, background, family structure, etc., that keep her from growing in faith."[4]

How do you start a cell group, for example among Muslims? What type of study materials would you use? I start every Muslim who comes to me with the basics. If you build a house, you dig four main foundations. I use the *Four Spiritual Laws* translated and adapted into Arabic to begin this spiritual house. Amazingly, Muslims respond as readily as traditional Christians to these simple transferable concepts. This is available also in Hebrew. I find it wise to lead new Muslim believers in a study of the Sermon on the Mount in Matthew 5-7, since it lays the basic foundation for prayer and moral living. Those who respond favorably can continue with a study *New Beginnings*, a programmed discipleship series that takes the new believer through the new life in Christ, Bible study, prayer, and life in the world and the church. "New Beginnings" is an excellent programmed discipling course which has been used to disciple Muslim background believers who are literate. (Back to Jerusalem, pp. 186-7) Somewhere around lesson 15 of the 50 lessons they are ready to make a full commitment to Christ, or to leave the study. *New Beginnings* was first created in the Philippines, probably patterned after the successful church planting of Charles Brock. Brock designed a basic discipleship series, *Good News for You,* a pre-salvation study of the Gospel of John, and *I Have Been Born Again, What Next?* (A pre-church study for new believers) which are available in English, Arabic, Russian and other languages. [5]

Use of *New Beginnings* encourages participation by each person present. The programmed texts give a Bible verse and then a question with a blank. Each person takes a verse and gives the answer to the question. I found this breaks down the barriers between men, women, and children in the Muslim family. Otherwise, only the man will lead and learn. Patterned after my simple, indirect leadership, the man of the family can continue leading the study in my absence. Each person pays for his or her own programmed workbook, which covers most of the cost. Simple Bible chorus sheets with an accompanying cassette provide the music. These are easily memorized. Usually one of the children or young people leads out. At the end of each section of about twenty lessons, each person receives a simple certificate verifying their successful completion and the hours spent in study. One advantage of such studies in the Muslim sector is they can be identified to the outsider as a "study" rather than as a religious meeting. A word of caution; avoid using commentary except to answer specific questions. Let the Scripture speak for itself. Commentary can lead to dispute and confusion. Commentary models a level of sophistication that others may not be able to attain, therefore limiting its transferability.

New Beginnings is actually the foundation study of a series of discipleship tools that can be used to train and disciple new believers. *Survival Kit* is another discipleship tool my wife used successfully in discipling English speaking Jewish ladies in Galilee. More advanced believers can study *Masterlife which* is available in the major local languages.

The True Furqan is a recently published book that can be used as an effective tool for pre-evangelism with Muslims. It uses Quranic Arabic and vocabulary to critique the Quran and popular Muslim attitudes toward Jesus and ethical living. *The True Furqan* is becoming increasingly noticed by Muslim leaders and will soon be available on the Internet.[6] I have been warned by Mbbs to be cautious in the use of the True Furqan as it has attracted much media attention in Arab countries.

You might ask, "Is it legitimate to use the Quran in discipling Muslim background believers?" Personally, I feel that the Bible is the best textbook for discipling them. Knowledge of the Quran and key verses and concepts is valuable in adapting the Biblical stories to Muslim thought forms. The Quran is more valuable as a bridge to witness. The stories of Mary and the virgin birth can be bridges to the Gospel accounts in Matthew and Luke. If you know the Quran well, as many Muslim background believers do, it can be used to point out that the Quran respects the Bible and the biblical prophets, therefore dispelling the violent polemic that Muslims and Christians sometimes fall into. You must be aware that the Quran contains contradicting verses which can bring confusion. The Muslim will assume that the Bible also contradicts itself, but will be amazed at the overall consistency of the Bible text.

An excellent witness-discipleship tool using the Bible and the Quran was designed by the late Fouad Accad, a Lebanese pastor and scholar. He incorporated verses from the Torah, Psalms, Gospels and the Quran to present the entire plan of salvation to a Muslim in Arabic. His book explaining this method has been published by the Navigators, *BUILDING BRIDGES, Islam and Christianity.*[7] Here are the very interesting and comprehensive "Seven Muslim-Christian Principles" which are listed in Appendix I

PRINCIPLE ONE: God Has a Purpose for Our Lives
PRINCIPLE TWO: Sin Separates Us from God
PRINCIPLE THREE: We Can't Save Ourselves
PRINCIPLE FOUR: The Cross Is the Bridge to Life
PRINCIPLE FIVE: God's Provision Is a Person
PRINCIPLE SIX: Making Him Ours
PRINCIPLE SEVEN: What to Expect When We Accept God's Gift.

My friend Hamdi used to visit me every Friday morning. I decided rather than waste our time on small talk that I would take him through the Seven. The lessons were too long to do in one sitting, so we divided each lesson in half. For over 14 weeks he came faithfully and read through all the Scriptures of each of the Principles. At the very end of the study there is a place to confess Christ as Savior and Lord. My friend read the statement which said, "I, (so and so) give my whole life to Christ Jesus to be my personal Savior and Lord." He made a point of reading it "so and so." I told him, "You are supposed to say, "I Hamdi give my whole life to Christ Jesus to be my personal Savior and Lord." He said, "Oh, I did that years ago!" Accad found that 80% of the Muslims who completed this study put their trust in Christ, so it is an effective method of pre-evangelism as well as an effective discipling tool. The *Seven Christian-Muslim Principles* provide a resource for those who want to use a "contextualized" approach to those Muslims who can only be reached through the use of the Quran. This tool, developed for the Navigators in Lebanon in Arabic and English, presents a topical study of the plan of salvation using verses from the Bible and the Quran. The seven lessons can be divided to use as a fourteen lesson series. Those who are not comfortable using the Quran may prefer not to use this tool. I found that many verses in the Quran emphasize man's depravity and God's judgment and combined with Bible verses can speak to the heart of some Muslims.

The *Camel Training Manual* has become a popular approach to witness and discipleship of Muslims. It uses the Quran to explain the message of salvation. It is highly contextualized for the Muslim who lives in a conservative community and has been effective in some Southeast Asia countries. A similar approach using a conversation between Muslim friends was designed by a MBB entitled *The Belief of Isma'il*.[9] These methods show us that God can use Quran as a bridge to faith. The objective is to get the Muslim to read the Scriptures which will enable him or her to distinguish the truth and apply it to their lives.

The subjects of service and stewardship should be among the content of discipling Muslim background believers. We should encourage the Muslim believer in bi-vocational leadership. They should keep their jobs and remain among their families in order to provide support for the Muslim believer's movement. Islam spread worldwide though Muslim merchants who married local women, in addition to the preaching and teaching of the Sufi missionaries. The Muslim believer's movements worldwide can use these indigenous models, clarified by the teaching of the Scriptures and the example of Paul and the early disciples in planting self supporting believer's churches in their society. I lived in the village of Josephus for about five years. One day I was amazed to see a group of Sufi's walking down the main street of this predominant Christian town. The leader, dressed in robes and a turban, much similar to what I would picture Jesus wore, strode with bold and deliberate steps, pounding his walking stick on the pavement, and his disciples following beside and behind him. They were part of the modern Islamic *da'wah* movement that itinerates in the towns of the Holy Land calling Muslims back to prayer and devotion to Allah.

Many Muslims, particularly women, come to Christ from a background of fearing God, evil spirits, the evil eye, envy of others and ritual uncleanness. The content of discipleship should emphasize their identity in Christ, their position of wholeness, cleanness, and total acceptance by God who reveals his love for us through the shed blood of Christ and the continual cleansing and regeneration of the Holy Spirit.[10]

We also must prepare Muslim background believers to face persecution and martyrdom. To teach them all the positive aspects of the Gospel and not prepare them for possible mistreatment at the hands of their family and society is not to deal honestly with them. They will thrill at the story of the spread of the Gospel in the Book of Acts. Acts is the textbook for a church planting movement among the Muslim unreached people groups worldwide.

We can trust the Holy Spirit and the Word of God to lead Muslims in the development of culturally appropriate believers groups, or churches. We must allow them to develop their own ecclesiology, while acquainting them with ours. In most cases they will chose the ecclesiology of those who disciple and mentor them. We will look now at forming congregations or affinity groups.

Endnotes: Chapter 5

[1] Four Spiritual Laws, Campus Crusade for Christ, available in various languages through the Internet, www.campuscrusade.com

[2] "Sin of Smoking" available in many languages from: ALL NATIONS GOSPEL PUBLISHERS, P.O. Box 2191, Pretoria, 0001, R.S.A.

[3] Christine A. Mallouchi, *Waging Peace on Islam,* p. 205.

[4] A.H. op.cit. Those who want to learn more about Chronological Bible Storying should consult the website: www.choronologicalbiblestorying.com.

[5] Church Growth International, 13174 Owens Lane, Neosho, MO 64850, USA.

[6] *The True Furqan*, WinePress Publishing, Enumclaw WA 98022, 1999 or from asea777@truth-in-crisis.com

[7] Fouad Elias Accad, *BUILDING BRIDGES, Christianity and Islam,* Bridges of Peace International (NavPress), 1997, pp.71-137.

CHAPTER 6

FORMING AFFINITY GROUPS

Muslims, particularly of Middle East background, are a group and family oriented people. The individual Muslim receives their identity from his or her family, clan, and nation. Islam capitalized on this group cohesion and called Muslims, "the best of nations" or *khayr al ummah* in Arabic.[1] Group or clan loyalty requires total dedication. To leave Islam is to leave the family group which gives a Muslim their identity. Islam maintains a tight control over its adherents through physical, mental and spiritual bonds. There is no back door out of Islam. There is only a door to enter Islam. To leave is to become a *murtad*, or backslider who has returned to paganism and gone astray. The only alternative is to return to Islam or face the death penalty. A system of scolding, threats, bribery, sexual enticement or deprivation, exclusion, job loss, and finally death by starvation, poisoning or stabbing has been devised to insure that backsliders return to the fold.

All of the above are good reasons to encourage Muslim background believers to remain in their family or clan in order to quietly influence their spouses, children, relatives and friends to receive the Gospel and be saved. The old method of requiring a Muslim background believer to declare publicly his faith in Christ resulted in "extraction" of the believer to save his or her life. It meant having to provide them with a new family and occupation, and many times a new country. This is usually the case when a teenage Muslim receives Christ and their conversion becomes a point of rebellion against the authority of his parents. There are cases where extraction cannot be avoided, but we are finding that most Muslims have trusted friends and family members who will quickly share the joy of their new faith in Jesus. If they remain respectful of their parents and spouses and leaders of their family and clan they can slowly influence many of them to read the Bible and to discover personally the truth that they have found. Lifestyle changes cannot be hidden and this causes others to seek out the source of their new life.

Always pray for the Lord to lead you to the man and woman of peace in a household. Until there is a leader of the family who is a believer it is very difficult for a younger person to assert their faith. This is not a hard and fast rule, for there are some Muslim families who have tolerant parents or leaders who know that the Gospel of Christ is a good thing for their members to hear. The problem comes when the news gets out to the community and the family leader is pressured to take action against the believer in order to preserve the reputation of the family. This is one reason that Christian schools have a vital ministry in Muslim countries. A wise Muslim parent can send their children to a Christian school since it provides a quality education and chance for a better future for their children. The winners in Bible memory contests in the Christian school in our Middle Eastern town were Muslims, since they already practiced the memorization of the Quran which gave them good practice.

Baptism is the decisive turning point for an inquirer or seeker to become identified as a Muslim background believer. What we may think of as "secret baptism" is not really secret when one Muslim baptizes another Muslim and some of their family and friends are there. Those who have been baptized gather naturally into their family or friendship groups. They protect each other and provide for each other's physical and social needs. The timing of a Muslim background believer's baptism should be the prerogative of the man or woman of peace who won them to the Lord and is discipling them. I know of many occasions when Barnabas told me that a person he was discipling was not ready for baptism. It often involved a lack of comprehension of the Gospel and the security issue. We have had people who join the believer's movement to spy out other believers either for the local government security services or for the fundamentalist Muslim movements. Sometimes a Muslim's baptism is delayed until they can lead other family members or friends to the faith and join them to establish a believers group. In most cases, baptism gives new courage to the Muslim background believer and the Holy Spirit empowers him or her to grow stronger in their faith.

Nik Ripken observed through many interviews with Mbbs, that their chief concern was: "Have I been baptized into Christ and into a new community?" They are seeking a home, a place to belong and a community that will care for their spiritual and physical needs. Baptism is community, local and eternal. They likely will be baptized multiple times and pass through many foreign expatriate organizations in the search for real community. MBBs can practice baptism as symbol, sign and sacrament within the same family in one generation. Few Muslims find Christ in a vacuum, apart from some type of church around them. Interviews illustrate Muslim men who have been on a spiritual journey for years. They have experienced Christ through dreams, visions and miracles. God has miraculously placed His Word in the seekers' hands. Some near-culture believer enters the picture to help these seekers understand what they have read, dreamed and sought. After three to seven years of searching, these Muslims find Christ and are eventually baptized. Their baptism is a symbol of their new life in Christ. Still influenced by their Muslim background and male self-image, they carry a witness to their wives. Surrounded by different Christian faith systems, it is not unusual for these MBB men to baptize their wives in three to six months.

These women were baptized because their husbands unduly influenced them, not because of a spiritual conviction arising from personal faith. It is surprisingly common for these MBB men to then baptize their infant child. They have viewed various denominations and their practices. They are not willing to take the chance that baptism itself might not provide salvation. Infant baptism also appeals to the residue of Islam within them, which suggests that faith is a result of external practices. In numerous interviews with MBBs, neither the wife nor the children could articulate the role of Jesus in salvation. When doctrinal practices precede faith, Christianity has a difficult task moving into and through succeeding generations. Baptism is not the primary debate here, though it is central to community. It is meant to be illustrative. In the presence of numerous Christian faith systems, baptism can travel from symbol, to sign, to sacrament in one generation. Such practices are due to observed behavior and imported doctrinal differences. An intentional effort will need to be made to return baptism to New Testament roots of identification with Christ, centered within families and local community.[2]

The family becomes the ideal setting for a house church fellowship or congregation in a Muslim setting. This can happen in countries with mixed Muslim and Christian populations and where religious freedom is practiced. A Muslim family is usually an extended family with the aunts and uncles, nephews and nieces sharing meals with each other. It is not uncommon for one or two in each family to be "religious" and to practice daily prayers as Muslims. Also, if the leader of the family is a believer he can have private meetings with other believers who come to visit, since he has the power to demand privacy. Men often meet for their own business at nights, to talk and drink coffee. They know how to keep secrets, and are cautious around people they suspect as informers. Women also have their own gatherings in other parts of the house or courtyard and the children usually stay with them.

We have had believers groups form in villages and rent their own place to meet. They usually use the place during the day as a kindergarten or some other legitimate community service activity. The meeting place is used in the evenings for teaching sessions and worship. The only difficulty is when a group becomes too prominent and becomes a threat to the established Muslim political leadership in the community. It is then that the meeting place is usually torched, and the houses of believers can be burned. In secure areas we now have house churches where the leaders from surrounding towns meet on a weekly basis for Bible study and prayer, and the breaking of bread.

Student fellowships form naturally on campuses where Muslim background believers attend college together. We had one group that became so large it became a threat to the Muslim student organization on campus. Our leader had to intervene to guarantee that the believers group would not compete with the Muslim religious group. Despite this, the believing student leader was murdered during a demonstration on campus. He was drug out of the office where he had fled, was pronounced a *kafir* or infidel and stabbed to death. Despite persecution, students who are believers become the leaders of other groups as they return to their home communities or to other areas for jobs. It is recognized that student groups only last as long as the believing students are studying on campus, and are in a constant state of flux.

Many Muslims work away from home, and in other countries. Muslim background believers gather in their work locations for meetings and Bible study. They often find more freedom when away from home and have time to study the Bible without distraction in their off hours. There was a resort town in our country that had a large Muslim workers community. A Muslim background believer who was a law student became the leader of the believers group in the resort area where he had to work to make money for school.

His uncle was the leader of the believers in his home town in another part of the country. Muslim background believers take their faith with them to other locations when they have to move. We try to network them with other believers in their work locations. This follows the popular pattern of the spread of Islam by Muslim merchants throughout the Middle and Far East, and all over the world today.

A Great Commission Christian partner has a very successful ministry among Muslim women in a city with a large refugee population. They rent a house dedicated to prayer in the name of Jesus with the permission of the wife of the President of the country and the protection of their security services. Women come for food rations, and for Bible study and prayer. The Lord has given signs of blessing through healings and divine intervention in a hostile political environment. The local government protects this house and its activities as a matter of religious liberty. Three to five hundred Muslims have been baptized through this ministry. They now have home meetings throughout the city. A retired Christian pastor and his wife who have a heart for Muslims lead some of their Bible studies.

My personal opinion is, that where two or three Muslims gather in the name of Jesus, he is in their midst. I call this an "embryo church." It can be in a car, under a tree, in a field, a shop, or a house. It is a spiritual church and the Lord blesses it with his presence. We have to free ourselves of the Byzantine view of a church building and clergy who alone can share the sacraments. We must disciple Muslim background believers to gather their family and friends whom they can trust and study the Bible with them. We must train them to pray for their individual and group needs, for healing from their illnesses and courage to face persecution. The Lord answers these prayers often in miraculous ways.

There are Muslim countries which have experienced upheaval and invasion by other Muslims countries. One such county in South East Asia has seen tens of thousands of Muslims turn to Christ as a reaction to the rape of their women by an invading Muslim army. The movement has grown so large they are now experiencing the denominational problems Christian countries face. When we disciple Muslim background believers in Christ, we must help them to be as tolerant as Jesus was toward his wayward disciples, and to love each other. We must resist importing our denominational infighting to our Muslim believers. They will mimic our ecclesiology and our denominationalism. What a blessing when we seen them worshiping across denominational barriers and ministering to each other and to believers from other faith backgrounds. We want to see Christ reflected in them personally and communally. The community of Muslim background believers becomes the church within the Muslim community to permeate their society with the love of Christ through word and deed.

Contextualization is usually involved as Muslim background believers seek to harmonize opposing world view systems so that the believers can survive within their Muslim religious and cultural system. One expatriate worker among Muslims has observed:

"Fundamentally it is local believers finding ways for themselves to exist peacefully within a hostile host culture. Not being told how to do it by people who could escape the consequences...I spent a long time listening to believers thinking out loud as to how they could "work it out" without compromising their faith. In the end I concluded that it was they who had to establish the terms because they had to live by them even though some went to the point where they could not associate with Western Christians, something which I have great difficulty with and which caused me much sadness.[3]

There has been endless discussion over how far Muslim background believers can go in adapting the Gospel message to the Islamic world view and culture of their specific country. A scale of C-1 to C-5 has been created to describe the various levels of adaptation or rejection of the host culture. The more a Muslim background believer and his fellowship group adapts to the local Islamic world view, the further away from the Christian culture view they move.

One worker among Muslims observed that most of those who joined his movement quit praying in the Mosque and started to read the Bible years ago. To go back to a worship forms similar to that of their former life would be seen as a step backwards. Perhaps the real issue was the trend in their society in general to adapt more western forms of meetings for study and prayer, rather than the rituals of Muslim prayer. I observed that regardless of the styles of worship, most Muslim believer groups have been reluctant to be too closely associated with the Arab Christian groups in their area. They tend to stick to their own society except for a few individuals who cross over into the Christian culture, and these are usually Muslims who have married Christian women.

What are the changes that we should expect from our Muslim background believer in the discipling process, as Christ is formed in them? We shall look at the changes that result in the next chapter.

Endnotes: Chapter 6

[1] Quran 3:110

[2] Nik Ripkin, *Servants in the Crucible,* p. 26.

[3] "Jameel", specific people group omitted for security

CHAPTER 7

CHANGES THAT RESULT

The experience of one who disciples, mentors and counsels Muslim background believer is similar to that of Paul who claimed it is like having labor pains until the Christ was formed in the Galatians.[1] Discipling and counseling Muslim background believers is time consuming and demands great patience and flexibility. As we saw in the beginning, Muslims come to faith with lots of baggage, misconceptions, and fears. You will have many times of frustration and bewilderment. At least you know that when you see lifestyle changes in the Muslim background believer, that God is working in their lives. We have to relieve ourselves of the burden of feeling we are totally responsible for the relapses and the errors of our disciples. Our obligation is to teach them, model for them and pray for them on condition that they pass on what they learn from us to others. We also have an obligation, when possible, to observe those they are discipling in order to coach them in the discipling process.

The man of peace I was discipling, Barnabas, was very insistent that we read the Scriptures and pray every time we met. I learned through this experience that he was reading large portions of Scripture very fast as Arabs often do. He was not concentrating or meditating on the meaning of the passages. His wife and other believers confirmed that he was doing this. They were getting bored by the long readings. I then showed him how to read shorter passages and to concentrate on the meaning of the wording and their relation to other passages. I also helped him to use life applications and cross references to make the Scripture relevant to his disciples. He later took pride in showing me how he read and interpreted the Scripture for others.

I also was under the leadership of another colleague in my organization who counseled me in my role as a team leader and mentor of Muslim background believers. He often asked me how my friend Barnabas was growing in his faith. I honestly told him that Barnabas was having some problems with money and persecution. My colleague then told me that he felt better hearing this, because if everything was going too well he could not trust the report! He had enough experience relating to Muslim background believers that he knew they had a rocky road to travel on the way toward spiritual maturity.

Barnabas was a chain smoker when he first came to me to ask to be taught the faith. He had three wives at that time and I use to say that he smoked three packs of cigarettes a day; one for each wife! He was constantly broke and having to pull deals on people to get extra money. I told him that as long as he smoked he would remain poor and his health would suffer. In fact, he had several heart attacks and finally had to have bypass surgery. The medications he was required to take made smoking even more dangerous for his health. I used the "Sin of Smoking" tract with him in our discipleship process along with the Four Spiritual Laws and regular Bible study, prayer and worship with other believers. As he began to understand the faith better he slowly cut down on the cigarettes and after his bypass surgery he quit, despite occasional relapses. I insisted on honesty, and had a very good nose for smoke since my mother had been a chain smoker. His friends would often tell on him if he smoked. I told him that believers did not lie. We had to be totally honest with each other if I was going to take the time to disciple him. One day after a particularly difficult time with persecution, bad health and finances he hung his head and said, "Despite all my problems, I have learned one thing." I asked him, "What?" He said, "To tell the truth!"

On another occasion I was riding in his car with him. I noticed to my surprise, empty beer bottles rattling around in the floorboard. I asked him if he had been drinking. He said, "You drink. So I thought there was nothing wrong with it!" Then I realized that when he visited my home he had seen empty malt beer bottles. This is a non-alcoholic drink made in my host country which is a health drink and tastes sweet like Pepsi Cola. I had to explain that we normally did not consume alcoholic beverages, and especially when we were driving! The experience impressed on me how much the Muslim background believer observes us and our lifestyle in the discipling and mentoring process. Muslims sometimes assume that all Christians drink alcoholic beverages, which is contrary to Muslim teaching. This can give opportunity for a study of the Biblical instructions concerning excess and drunkenness and the responsibility of a believer to set an example for weaker believers.

Character formation is an essential part of the discipling and mentoring process. Muslim background believers have to deal with many issues that impact on their character and their witness to others. We have already discussed the issue of polygamy. The Muslim believer needs to understand the spiritual motivation behind monogamy, that is; Christ's love and devotion to the Church who is his spiritual bride. The instruction of the Scripture and the inspiration of the Holy Spirit will guide him and his wives in solving this delicate family issue. In the two cases of Muslim background believers who had multiple wives before they came to the faith, both arranged equal provisions for all their wives and lived with the youngest. The matter of divorce is not a real solution, since it turns the divorced wife out of the home and makes her dependant on her family, disgracing her, and could lead a woman to resort to prostitution. On the other hand, if the unbelieving wife divorces her believing husband, he has no alternative but to give her back her dowry and pay for child support. Whatever is done in the case of polygamy, the best interests of the wife and children should be taken into consideration. If dealt with sensitively and wisely, with good relations in the multiple families affected, it can lead to the rest of the family receiving the Lord and their spreading the faith among their relatives and friends.

The situation is made more problematic when a Muslim background believer takes a new wife after coming to faith in Jesus. In every case it causes difficulties in relation to the first wife and her children. We have had to exercise discipline and exclude the husband from fellowship. In some cases he returns to the mosque as a way to get back at us. I have known Muslim background believers, or those pretending to be believers, to pull all kinds of tricks to manipulate others to satisfy their own lust and pride. Fortunately, these have been the exception rather than the rule. In reality, expatriates need to be aware that this is not as big an issue in the Muslim community as it is for us. Whereas monogamy has always been our accepted standard, multiple marriages and divorces is the practice of the Muslim community. I am not justifying polygamy, simply observing the major difference in our way of life. Muhammad had multiple wives and concubines, similar to our Old Testament prophets and he allowed Muslim men to marry up to four women at one time, if he could treat each one equally. Muslims jokingly say that he really meant for them to stay monogamous, since a husband naturally will favor one wife over the others!

Cursing is a definite problem for Muslims. In our country, where another language was spoken, if a person wanted to really express themselves, they would curse in Arabic! The Arabic language is noted for its color and descriptiveness. Little boys curse their sisters and mothers and the men laugh. Gutter language is a way of life. Unmentionable body parts and functions flavor expletives. Cursing a person's mother or sister is par for the course. The "F" word is used in Arabic almost as much as the name of Allah. You know the Lord is beginning to work in the inner man when a Muslim background believer begins to clean up his language.

Unfortunately what comes out of the mouth often results from a boiling cauldron of pent-up hostility and anger in the heart which can burst out at the least provocation. I have seen Muslim men stop cars in the street and begin fighting each other. In one case a man ran into a local butcher shop, grabbed a knife and stabbed another driver to death. The least provocation can set off a reaction to settle old grudges. Islam is a religion that tries to control man's evil tendencies by a rigid set of rituals and lifestyle rules that are practiced 24 hours a day. When a Muslim comes to the Lord, and the pressure of these rituals and rules are relaxed, they need guidance and discipline in living the new life in Christ. They must be taught to put on the whole armor of God every day, to guard against the strategy of the Devil to drag men and women down to the level of predatory animals.

My friend Barnabas had a teenage son who was slightly mentally retarded. He had lost oxygen in childbirth and his mother had almost died delivering him. As he grew older and bigger he became more difficult to handle. One day Barnabas struck the boy. He went to school and his teacher noticed the bruise. She called the police and had Barnabas arrested. He was humbled by the experience of the few hours behind bars and the threat of long term imprisonment if he hit the boy again. We were able to use this as a growth opportunity by praying for patience and studying scripture related to controlling one's temper. The boy also became more obedient and started listening to the reading of the Word.

In the process of mentoring, discipling and counseling with Muslim background believers you can expect the Lord to discipline them, as well as impart the fruit of the Spirit of love, joy, peace, patience, and kindness. There will be lapses, as there is with all of us. It is very difficult when believers backslide and return to their vomit. We had three leaders who betrayed us. Two are now dead, having faced the judgment of God for their actions. The third is now the representative of his government in a foreign country. He evidenced some repentance before he left and we pray the Lord will redeem him. For every one who backslides, ten will remain faithful to the Lord. We have seen them share their faith with other, their wealth, and even their lives as martyrs for Him. Through all the ups and downs of the discipling process, God is building a body from thousands of Muslim background believers worldwide. It is a beautiful experience to see the Lord change the hearts of Muslims to the place they can love their enemies and even witness to them to bring them to the faith.

Mert Hershberger refers to the stages of spiritual growth illustrated in Jesus' parable of the growth of wheat in Mark 4:17. The new believer must die to self in order to put down roots of faith. Then they extend the stem toward the light of the Lord. The third stage of spiritual growth involves development of a head of grain for reproduction. Then the full head of grain appears representing the gifts of the Spirit in Galatians 5:22-23. Finally, the harvest gathers the ripe grain into the storehouse, where it can then be used to produce the bread, which is symbolic of the one loaf and wedding feast of the King and his Bride, the church. Paul, the missionary expands on the stages of spiritual growth in Romans 5:1-5. Faith leads to hope of the goal of the Glory of God revealed in the life of the believer. It is achieved by enduring troubles and sufferings which produce character and endurance. This hope does not disappoint us because of the love of God which is poured out in our hearts through the Holy Spirit which has been given to us. Hershberger goes on to analyze the teachings of James, Peter and John describing how testing, trials, and needs issue in wisdom and the indwelling presence of God in the growth process. Character and self control is developed as the believer seeks the help of God in prayer and grows from a child in faith, to an adolescent, and finally to a reproductive adult who has stood the tests of their faith.[2]

Those disciplers or mentors of Pentecostal persuasion would add to the above list of changes and change agents in the Muslim background believer's growth in Christ, the baptism in or of the Holy Spirit. I come from a tradition that normally adheres to the giving of the Holy Spirit to the new believer when they first accept Christ. Most of the Baptist tradition will maintain that a believer receives all he or she needs from the Spirit at the time of accepting Christ as savior. Therefore, they are suspicious of the necessity for a second "baptism" in the Spirit with the expectation of manifestations such as tongues. I personally believe the Holy Spirit is the active agent throughout the discipling process and manifests Himself through the new believer in a variety of ways. Certainly we want to give freedom to the Spirit to operate anyway He chooses in the growth of spirituality and maturity of the Muslim background believer. I have found them very open to accept all the Lord offers in the way of gifts, prayers for healing and other spiritual manifestations. They are especially open to dreams, visions, and what would be called miracles of healing, simply because of their spiritual world view. The Book of Acts is our best handbook of the changes we would like to see in the life of Muslim background believers, and the Epistles contain all that is needed for regulating and channeling these changes for the glory of God.

We need to distinguish between those changes required by the Word of God through the Holy Spirit and those changes which are a reflection of our own culture. In the past the "extraction" method of conversion was advocated which effectively cut a Muslim background believer off from his family and culture. Christine Mallouchi reports that when her husband, Mazhar Mallouchi responded to God's call in the 1950's, "he was told that he needed to leave his old sinful life behind. He needed to change his name; stop drinking in coffee shops; refuse to join his family's religious celebrations; stay away from mosques; stay away from Muslims; stop fasting; pray with a different posture, and eat pork to prove he was converted. It was not surprising that his family angrily opposed his conversion and he soon no longer had any relationships with his old friends who he had rejected. He experienced a terrible identity crisis and total dislocation from his culture, family and friends. In spite of this he was still not totally accepted by the Christian community. Christine goes on to clarify that the New Testament states clearly the 'the Kingdom of God is not a matter of food and drink, but righteousness and joy in the Holy Spirit.' Moreover it tells us to stay put in the communities where Christ finds us." She goes on to clarify that,

> "As we share our faith with others it is vitally important to understand that our religious traditions are not the Gospel and may actually have little relationship to the Gospel message and even be obscuring it. Following Christ does not mean joining the *Christian* culture that has grown up over the centuries. It does not require leaving one's family and people. To follow Christ does not require one to take a new *Christian* name, or to wear a different style of clothing. Nor does it require using the symbol of the cross, nor worshipping on a certain day, nor a certain style of worship–...The only reason we may need to change any of these practices—in any culture of the world—is if there is a direct link with sin or Satan. Then there is a need to beware of confusing culture and religion... So what does it mean to believe in and follow Christ? The one thing following Christ requires is to believe his words about himself—that he is the Word of God bringing us back into unbroken

communication with God...We have to die to self in order to walk in holiness; to follow God's command, 'Walk with me and be perfect.' It means to enter into a new relationship with the living Christ, to learn from him and obey his commands for living a life pleasing to God. It means acceptance of his other followers as family members."[3]

Those of us from a culturally Christian background need to ask, "What is our role in assisting Muslim background believers in growing into the image of Christ." That will be the theme of the next section.

Endnotes: Chapter 7

[1] Galatians 4:19

[2] Mert Hershberger, *Steps toward Maturity: NT Models for the Stages of Spiritual Growth,* World Christian Foundations: Module 2, William Carey International University (n.d)

[3] Christine A. Mallouchi, *Waging Peace on Islam,* pp. 323-325.

CHAPTER 8

ROLE OF THE EXPATRIATE MENTOR

Your role as an expatriate church planter in the discipling process with a Muslim background believer will change during the various stages of spiritual growth of the believer. You may or may not be the first person who gave a witness to the Muslim. In most cases there have been a series of persons or experiences that the Lord has used to bring the Muslim to a position of faith in Jesus as their savior. Their willingness to be discipled by you is an indication that God has been working in their lives. Muslims are usually very determined to win you to their faith, and the simple fact that they are willing to learn from you can be considered an act of divine intervention. God may have used problems, dreams, visions, curiosity, or even envy to arouse the Muslim's desire to learn more about Jesus. Some even come to the point of wanting to know more about Jesus through a study of the Quran. Others come through a rejection of the hypocrisy they see in the Mosques where they pray. Many come from a thirst for love and trust which is lacking in their home cultures.

In the beginning you will want to know their background and exposure to the Gospel. It is very easy to jump ahead of the leadership of the Holy Spirit and omit a necessary stage in the development of the spiritual maturity of the Muslim background believer. Perhaps it is best not to assume anything, but to begin with the basics. If the Muslim is not an English speaker you will need to learn their language and culture. A basic knowledge of Arabic is always a good tool in relating to the Quran. A course in Islam will prove helpful in understanding their background and culture. Cultural studies on the influence of the occult and syncretism in the specific Muslim culture will be very helpful.

Your role in the beginning may be that of a witness, then a teacher, counselor and mentor. An integral part of every discipling role is that of prayer partner and guide. In the end you may maintain the role of an advocate for their work among their own people. Friendship and trust are key elements in your role as a spiritual guide to a Muslim background believer. Since many Muslims will be unaware of how Christians live their life in Christ, lifestyle witness and mentoring are essential in your role.

Bill Hull elaborates on four stages of training through which Jesus took his disciples. First, he told them to "come and see" what his ministry was like for a four month period as recorded in John 1:35-4:46. Secondly, he called them to "come and follow me" during ten months of observation and learning, beginning in Mark 1:16-17. Eventually, he said, "Come and be with me," as an invitation to a twenty month period of practical ministry experience in Matthew 9:37-10:1. Finally, Jesus told his disciples on the night he was betrayed, "You will remain in me," as he began to relate the way they would carry out his Great Commission in John 13-17.[1] Jesus did not expect his disciples to learn everything at one time, but shared with them in stages as they grew in spiritual maturity and could handle it. The process was not completed until they were filled with the Holy Spirit and empowered on and after Pentecost. This led all to be bold witnesses and many to suffer martyrdom. Such is the ideal progression for Muslim background believers.

Our problem as disciplers, mentors and counselors of Muslim background believers is being willing to commit the time to impart all this spiritual training and formation to our Muslim friends who are asking to be discipled. It is time and labor intensive. We have to be willing to give up some of the activities that drain our time, and many of these are with Christian churches and friends. We can be so busy being Christians and keeping our various churches and organizations going that we do not take the opportunity to really spend the quality time that discipling Muslims demands. I simply had to forego some church meetings and mission committees to give my Muslim friends the time they needed to be with me to learn from me. Some of the modeling they need can only be accomplished in the presence of our wives and other Christian friends. Jesus was willing to spend two to three years of intensive fellowship with his disciples to prepare them for the Cross and the filling of the Holy Spirit after the resurrection. We need to be willing to do the same. My friend Barnabas spends from one to three years with a Muslim background believer to bring them to the maturity of leadership.

The ideal is for a local Muslim background believer to disciple other Muslim believers. Nevertheless, in the beginning of a work it may be necessary for someone from outside the culture, that is, an expatriate, to come in and witness to and disciple new believers. Some local Christian believers will tell you that the Muslim is much more likely to listen to an outsider than to one of the local believers. Muslims may have a feeling of superiority over the local Christian population, especially if the Christians are in the minority. Also, an American or European is considered to be under the protection his government. Usually the worst he or she could suffer is expulsion from the host country. Whereas the local Christian believer could be the brunt of persecution were they to try to evangelize or disciple Muslims. This is not always the case as we have seen by the murder of numerous American missionaries in recent years in Muslim countries.

I personally feel it is important for the expatriate church planter and discipler to conform to the language and culture of the Muslims they are trying to reach and develop. To expect the local Muslim to learn English and bond to the expatriate may cause them to be cut off from their native culture. This would make it even harder for the Muslim believer to convince his own family and friends of the truth of the Gospel. We must do everything possible to allow the Gospel to take root in the language and culture of the Muslim background believer. As Bill Hull says in *New Century Disciplemaking,* "The disciple must be taught by both example and explanation how to reach the lost where they live, work and play—in the real world."[3] We do not necessarily have to adopt Muslim religious and cultural forms, but we can use them as bridges to enhance the understanding of the Gospel.

Counseling Muslim background believers may necessitate a different role from that of the typical western counselor. In the west most counseling is done in private and in confidentiality. Among many Muslim unreached people groups counseling is often done in group settings. In the case of a couple who is having marital problems, often the entire family is involved in the cause and the remedy of the problem. Family reputation is at stake and the entire family and clan may be involved in negotiating a solution. In any case, we as expatriates must maintain the confidence and trust of the parties involved. For sure, anything you share with an outside party will soon get back to the persons involved. You have to be very careful in expressing opinions about anyone, since you will often be talking to one of their relatives. Some people will try to get you to say things so that they can tell the other person and get you in difficulty with them. So, be careful.

Also, western counseling is often indirect and non-confrontational. In Muslim cultures, counseling is often direct, even though it must appear to be in the third person so as not to offend. Muslims and people of Middle East origin are used to corporal punishment, or the threat of it to enforce discipline on children and sometimes on adults. A wayward husband who beats his wife may need to be told that you will personally punish him if he hits her again. You can make it clear that you do not want your reputation tarnished by his actions, and that her family might be led to take revenge on him for his mistreatment of her. In most cases the face to face threat of physical punishment is enough to deter further mistreatment. Of course this should be accompanied with the teaching that husbands are to love their wives as Christ loved the Church and gave himself up for her.

The need to discipline or correct a Muslim background believer can be threatening to the expatriate who may fear rejection if they call an error to the attention of the disciple. This is not necessarily the result, as experienced by a female expatriate who was discipling a Muslim woman in France. She relates,

"For me the fear is of being rejected. If I really talk to these Muslim women about issues that need to be talked about, I fear they won't want me to visit again. Recently, I was in the home of a new believer who is experiencing many problems. I noticed she had an amulet around her neck that I had never seen before. I sat through the entire meeting thinking, "What am I going to do about this?" Yet I was afraid to talk to her about it, because I was afraid of the answer she was going to give. It would mean I had failed because I hadn't discipled her enough and she had reverted to trusting this thing to help her. But God wouldn't let me leave her home without asking about it. She explained it was a gift from her father. She was afraid not to wear it because he had given it to her. We studied Ephesians 6 and the next time I saw her, she wasn't wearing it." This worker admitted being afraid that her disciple may later regret having removed the amulet if some misfortune happened to her.[2]

I have found that counseling Muslims is a two way street. You can tell them your opinion on a matter, and give advice, or instruction. At the same time, they will observe your private life and reactions and call any deviation from your teachings to your attention. A good example will not go unnoticed as reported by Kay Waters, a health worker in North Africa. "If the family knows and trust us and sees our respect and love for their culture, and they perceive us as holy, God-fearing, hospitable, loving and generous people, they might be much less likely to reject the MBB. This may be particularly crucial for single women reaching out to unmarried daughters in Muslim families. We must be very careful not to be perceived as corrupting or destructive forces within the family." She notes a case in which the team leader was able to gain the respect of the key men in the family of one of the believing women, Lydia, who they were discipling. When some others in the family were pressuring Lydia to marry a Muslim man against her will, her colleague was able to share his concerns about the matter with the leading men of the family. Eventually he was accepted as a "surrogate uncle," and the other members of the family agreed to let him be responsible to counsel Lydia in this matter.[3]

As an expatriate we can share our testimony, read the Scriptures and pray with Muslim background believers. We can listen to their problems and complaints and share their victories. We need to bathe our relationship with them in prayer. In this way, we teach them to pray. They will ask for and expect our prayers when God calls us to another place. We can also build a prayer network to pray for our Muslim believer friends. We become their advocates as we share about their opportunities and the opposition they face.

A particularly sensitive aspect of the role of the expatriate in discipling and counseling Muslim background believers is the use of finances. Some expatriates will maintain a policy of not helping new Muslim believers financially under any circumstances. The motivation for this abstinence of financial aid is to prevent the Muslim believer from becoming dependant on the help of outsiders. The goal is worthy, but very difficult to put into practice in real life. I deal with the issue of financial support extensively in Chapter 4 of *Back to Jerusalem.*[4] The bottom line to me in discipling Muslim background believers is how to model love and wisdom in applying Jesus teachings in Matthew 5:42 and many other places to "Give to him who asks of you, and do not turn away from him who wants to borrow from you." Of course, if the expatriate simply does not have any money, then the problem is solved. But in most cases expatriate workers do have some ability to assist financially. This makes the situation more problematic. Many Muslims are in financial need because of their large families and due to deliberate persecution by their Muslim family and neighbors. Muslims are taught by tradition to visit, give gifts and to use material means to build friendship. A Muslim believer in financial need will naturally turn to his or her mentor as a first resort for help. I made it a practice not to carry large sums of money with me, so that any financial help would be kept to a minimum. I found it best not to lend money, since that places the Muslim background believer under an obligation that they may not be able to keep. It is always better to give a small gift than a large loan, which turns into a burden and barrier for both mentor and the Muslim background believer. Also, it is better to practice a "shared purse" where the Muslim believer provides a part of the need from his or her own resources. Better still, is to train them for a job that will remedy the financial need in the long run. I personally believe that partial scholarships provided to believing Muslim students is a good investment in the future.

One of the most important functions of the expatriate discipler, mentor, and counselor is to equip the Muslim background believer with the spiritual, mental, and social tools necessary to pass on their faith to others. Start early, in the beginning of the discipling process and trust the Word of God in the Scriptures and the Holy Spirit to empower and guide the Muslim believer in winning, baptizing and equipping other Muslim background believers. If we wait until they are mature, they may never get there!

One of the most important lessons we have to impart to the new believer is how to deal with persecution, which will surely come, if they are faithful to the Lord. Some will face martyrdom. Will they be prepared? This we will deal with in the following chapter.

Endnotes: Chapter 8

[1] Bill Hull, *New Century Disciplemaking,* pp. 221-222, quoted from Mert Hershberger, *Steps toward Maturity,* Endnotes, 1.

[2] Ministering to Muslim Women, *Longing to Call Them Sisters,* pp. 60-61.

[3] ibid, pp179-180.

[4] Ray Register, *Back to Jerusalem,* Church Planting Movements in the Holy Land, Wine Press, 2000, pp. 97-132 Critical Issues Examined—Danger! Land Mines!

CHAPTER 9

PREPARING FOR PERSECUTION AND MARTYRDOM

The reality of life as a believer in Christ, in this fallen world, is that they will suffer persecution, especially if they are a believer from Muslim background. An integral part of preparing a Muslim background believer to grow in Christ is preparing them for persecution and possible martyrdom. A Muslim who turns to Christ as Savior and Lord and becomes known to other Muslims for his or her faith is technically considered an unbeliever or *kafir*, and is subject to the death penalty as a backslider or *murtad* if they do not recant and return to Islam. Islam has a system of persuasions and punishments to persuade or force the Muslim background believer in Christ to renounce their faith or at a minimum to return to Islam and remain silent about their faith. First, they are warned and threatened. Then they are bribed. If they do not yield to offers of money, jobs, new wives, or husbands, then they can be attacked physically. Men can be beaten up, burned, robbed, their property destroyed, divorced by their wives, forced from their jobs, arrested by police under false charges, disinherited, and various other manipulative types of punishments. Women can be forced to marry unbelieving Muslims, or isolated, and slowly starved to death. Their children can be taken from them. In the end, if all else fails, they can be murdered by stabbing, strangling, poisoning or other methods. I have known Muslim background believers to survive for years in supposedly liberal countries, and then suddenly be killed during periods of political unrest.

"Mark" was a handsome, muscular young man, who married the beautiful niece of Lydia, our woman of peace. He became the driver of Barnabas, Lydia's husband and the leader of the Muslim background believers in our country. Mark did not take faith in Jesus seriously until one stormy night in the middle of the desert his car was forced off the road by fanatical Muslims, and overturned. He suffered multiple bruises, but Barnabas had numerous broken ribs and was in a coma for over a month in the hospital. I visited Mark after the accident to see what his reaction was. He told me, "I really did not take my faith seriously until the accident. Now I know that I have to be sold out for my faith in Jesus! Now I know what it means to be a believer." He started going to his hometown with Bibles and Gospel cassettes and videos and sharing his new faith with his family and friends. The other believers helped him get a loan to open up a business in town. One evening he received a desperate call that his mother and brothers were in serious trouble and he needed to come immediately. He closed the shop and took the money from the cash drawer with him. He was never seen again alive. After he had disappeared several weeks, his body was finally identified. It had been cut into three pieces. His beautiful wife was left with three small children. Her father, a policeman, buried Mark and told me, "Mark died because he had become a Christian." Now Mark's wife is being sued by the man who loaned him the money to open his business. To make matters even worse, the religious and political opposition put out word that he was not killed, but is still alive, causing both the believers and his family much distress.

"Steve" was the leader of a group of Muslim background believers who were students in a large Islamic University. They had used the "Sin of Smoking" tract and "Four Spiritual Laws" to lead a number of their friends to the Lord on campus. Their group grew so large that it began to compete with other political and religious groups on campus. On one occasion Barnabas went on campus to make a peace agreement or *sulha* between the rival groups. He encouraged the believers group to keep a lower profile and not to antagonize the non-believers. Things seemed to be going well until a political riot broke out on campus. Steve and some of the other believers took shelter in the school office since some in the administration had been sympathetic to their cause. The fanatic Muslims took advantage of the turmoil. They dragged Steve out of the office and stabbed him to death, screaming that he was a *murtad* and had left Islam.

"Paul" became a believer in his town. He donated his kidney to the leader of the women's group of believers in a nearby city. He grew quickly in the Lord. His house was burned, as well as the kindergarten, meeting place in his town. His son was standing beside the road early one morning waiting for a ride to work. A group of fanatics sped up and struck the boy with their car, leaving him with numerous broken bones. He is still recovering from his injuries. A teenage girl whose family is believers was severely burned when her home was firebombed by fanatics in the same area. She spent many weeks in the hospital for skin grafts. The story goes on and on.

The latest martyr was a young man who lived in a supposedly protected area. A group of fanatics forced his car off the highway into a cement bridge support and he was killed. When complaints were made to the police the believers were told they needed "proof." This and other cases convinced me that when a Muslim comes to faith in Christ he or she is signing their death warrant. We have to prepare new Muslim background believers not only to live for Christ, but to die for him.

Jesus taught his disciples that they are to be congratulated, or be blessed when they are persecuted for righteousness sake, and when people insult them and persecute them and falsely say all kinds of evil about them because of their faith in him. He promises the kingdom to them.[1] Paul promised Timothy that all who live a godly life in Christ Jesus will be persecuted.[2] This is certainly true of Muslim background believers. Mentors in Pakistan in *Longing to Call Them Sisters* report that "As we begin to witness to Muslim women, it's wise to say to them, "Not only is it given to you to believe on Christ, but also to suffer for his sake" (Phil. 1:29). Then they will understand that it is part of being a Christian. We've urged our people never to rush to tell their family about their profession of faith in Christ. Instead, we encourage them to live Christ before their family so that their family will have the opportunity to ask why they have changed... We've seen our young people threatened and beaten. Many of them have been threatened to have their limbs cut off or their arms broken. Some of them have been put out of their homes. Many of the women have been beaten. I don't know of any of our children who have escaped beatings in school. But we've taught them from 1 Peter 2:20: "If you do wrong and suffer for it, what is that to you? But if you do no wrong, but your suffering for Christ's sake, it is glory."[3]

I have known some Muslims who have kept their identity as Muslim background believers hidden, or low key, while remaining within the Muslim community. One of them who was a judge told me that it is best to send Muslim believers to another country to disciple them until they can become strong enough in the faith to be transplanted back into their home cultures. This has happened in some cases where Muslim believers have traveled abroad, studied, married and then returned to their home countries. The disadvantage of this is that they do not impact their families and friends during their discipling process. Also when they return they may be so westernized that their impact on the local community is marginalized. There is something about suffering inside the community which bonds the believers to others in the community. Even their enemies are impressed and some eventually come to the faith, similar to the experience of Saul who persecuted the church, but remembered the martyrdom of Stephen.

I do not advocate that Muslim background believers deliberately seek persecution and martyrdom. I counsel them to be cautious in relating their faith to other Muslims, until they can know that their message will be received. I somehow feel that their societies are so full of conflict as a normal way of life that they are more capable of suffering than those of us from western societies, where comfort is a premium.

If the Gospel can be shared by other Muslim background believers it will spread quicker among their own people. In some areas of the world, westerners and Christians in general can put Muslim background believers in danger just by being seen with them. Therefore it is better in some cases to meet with the leaders in a secure area, and train them to go back to their homes and businesses to share the Gospel in culturally sensitive ways with their families, associates and friends.

There was a well known evangelist who led twelve Muslims to the Lord. They were all killed. I asked him if he changed his discipling approach after this. He said, "Of course!" If he persisted in encouraging them in public profession of their faith in Christ, they would all be killed. He began to caution them to only share with other Muslims as the Spirit gave opportunities, and to do this in private after long testing. Each culture has its own norms and we need to advise our new believers to be aware of the dangers as well as the opportunities.

It is important that Muslim background believers be taught to memorize the Scripture in order to face persecution when neither the Bible nor other believers may be present to encourage them. The written or memorized Word of God is always present in their hearts to comfort and guide and to provide a witness to their persecutors. This need is enhanced through storying the Bible and through the memorization of Scripture choruses and hymns which are proven methods of discipling Muslim background believers who are oral communicators.

God is building the church among Muslims today. We will deal with the aspects of church planting as an integral part of the discipling process in the last chapter.

Endnotes: Chapter 9

[1] Matthew 5:10-11

[2] 2 Timothy 3:12

[3] *Longing to Call Them Sisters,* p. 137

[4] Bill Hull, *New Century Disciplemaking,* p.104.

CHAPTER 10

CARRYING THE GREAT COMMISSION TO OTHERS

More Muslims are accepting the salvation of Christ today than any other time in history. They are sharing their new faith in God's forgiveness for sins with their families and friends. Some are developing into evangelists who are proclaiming the Gospel to many around the world. The Great Commission applies to Muslim background believers as well as to believers from other backgrounds. In the Great Commission Jesus said, "All authority has been given to me in heaven and on earth. Go therefore and make disciples of all nations, baptizing them in the name of the Father and the Son and the Holy Spirit, teaching them to observe all that I commanded you; and lo, I am with you always, even to the end of the age."[1]

Every Muslim who takes his or her religion seriously is afraid of Hell fire. This fear is the chief motivating power of Islam. Muslim women are especially afraid of the final judgment. The Great Commission provides within it the message needed to help Muslims overcome this fear through faith in Christ. The setting of the final days of Jesus suffering, death, and resurrection was the Passover of the Jews which looked back to God's miraculous rescue of the Jews from the domination of Pharaoh through the sprinkling of the blood of the Passover lamb on the doorposts. Someone has organized the Great Commission witness into the "seven commandments of Jesus" which are very appropriate for sharing the Gospel with Muslims and enabling them to establish believing groups among other Muslims.[2]

These first three commandments are the beginning of the Muslim's pilgrimage to life in Christ. By obeying these three the Muslim personally enters the Kingdom, or the new *ummah* under the leadership of a new *Caliph,* the Lord Jesus Christ, who is the God-man redeemer of all men.

1.   Jesus commands them to **repent**. They must turn from their sins to God. This first commandment is the most basic, but often the hardest to accept and apply.

2.   Jesus commands them to **believe**. They must open their hearts to the Gospel of the Kingdom that Jesus paid the penalty for their sins. They must receive Him as personal Savior for the forgiveness of their sins. He is the Great Sacrifice offered for the sins of all men.

3.   Jesus commanded them to **be baptized**. Baptism by immersion in water symbolizes the death of the believer to sin and the resurrection to new life in Christ. It is the ceremonial door to the body of believers, the new *ummah.*

By keeping these next three commandments, the Muslim background believer takes part in the life of the community, or the Church.

4.   Jesus commanded them to **pray**. The simple prayer, "Our Father who art in heaven,,,," is the equivalent of the *fatiha* in Islamic prayer. It contains the basic elements of prayer for the new believer; adoration of God, request for his guidance, petition for our daily needs, the request for the forgiveness of sins, protection from temptation and evil and the affirmation of God's glory and reign over all men

5.   Jesus commanded them to **love one another**. Love is the motivating power of faith in Jesus. Love covers a multitude of sins. It is the distinguishing mark of the believer. God is love. Perfect love casts out all fear. This is the most difficult of Jesus commandments, since its power comes from complete dependence on the Spirit of God which Jesus places into the hearts of the believer. It is a supernatural quality which cannot be inspired by human action alone.

6.   Jesus commanded them to **remember him** through the Lord 's Supper.

      "Do this in remembrance of me," he commanded at the Passover meal, indicating the hidden Messiah unleavened bread or *matzah* and the Messiah cup which he fulfilled in his blood shed on the cross.

7.   The final commandment is **"you shall be my witnesses.**"[3] This is the commandment which benefits the world. Muslims are to bear witness in their Jerusalem, Samaria, and to the uttermost parts of the world. In this way they share Christ's salvation with their own people and with the people of the world. What better testimony to a Jew than a Muslim who has had their sins forgiven and forgives those who trespass against them!

      The above commandments are a simple method for Muslims to spread their faith to other Muslims and to start believing groups that multiply. We do not need complicated programs and doctrinal statements for Muslims to use in outreach. The Bible provides us with the simplest approach as well as the most effective approach. The Book of Acts of the Apostles serves as an excellent church planting manual for Muslim background believers.

Many methods are proving fruitful in reaching Muslims for Jesus. One is the use of the Internet. Muslims have many websites designed to entice Christians to become Muslims. Muslim background believers also have sites designed to share their faith with their Muslim brothers and sisters. One new site is being developed by the Academy of Theological Studies which used to enroll Arab professionals in Biblical studies. Those enrolled to study were invited to regional seminars which allowed students and professors to meet each other on a personal basis. Another group sponsored large regional Islamic study courses led by Christian scholars.

Distribution of the Jesus Film has been a primary way to share the Gospel with Muslims. This has been done by house to house visits which distribute pamphlets advertising the film. Those who respond are sent the film and later visited for follow-up. Sometimes newspaper advertisements offer the film or a copy of the Scriptures in the local language. A successful method of distributing Gospel Recordings audio cassettes and Wordless book among Bedouin Arabs resulted in many requests for the Jesus Film. A number of baptisms and believers groups resulted.

The goal of discipleship is not just to see Christ formed in the new believer but to have him glorified in believers groups or fellowships which produce other groups. Muslims are usually part of gregarious, family oriented societies. When they come to faith in Christ and begin to manifest the fruit of the Spirit, i.e. Love, joy peace, patience and the rest, it undoubtedly impacts their families, friends, business partners and the society around them. As more Muslims come to the Lord, they naturally gather daily or at least weekly to share and celebrate their faith together. Family celebrations and rites of passage become time of sharing about what God has done in their lives. Kay Waters excitedly reports in *Longing to Call Them Sisters* about a sister team who is seeing almost miraculous growth of a home related group. "They are discipling about 50 MBB's, virtually all of whom have come to faith within the last two years. Many of them came to the Lord as a result of the witness of their family members. Almost weekly we hear a report of someone else that has decided to follow Christ because they have been watching their family members or friends and seen their changed lives. The team does not need to seek out contacts with whom to share the gospel. The MBB's are continually bringing friends and family members to their homes so that they, too, can hear the good news!,,,Watching the growth of the church among this nearby Muslim people group, I am encouraged to see that the gospel really can spread through whole families!"[4] It is this kind of rapid, spontaneous multiplication that is the goal of discipling Muslims.

A natural way that Muslims reach out into their own communities is through the Sufi "way" or *tariqa.* The Sufis often went ahead of the Muslim armies that invaded new areas to soften up the attitude of the people of the area. They taught a contextualized form of Islam that was more acceptable to society. They incorporated local customs into their worship and prayers. Muslim background believers in Jesus can form their own "way" or *tariqa* which will adapt to those who have been chosen for salvation and include them into small groups.

Endnotes: Chapter 10

[1] Matthew 28: 18-20, NASV

[2] Dr. George Patterson, Seattle, Washington, idea received in Bible Study in Rancho Bernardo, April 30, 2004

[3] Acts 1:8

[4] Kay Waters, *Evangelism through Family Networks, Longing to Call Them Sisters,* pp. 186-187.

CONCLUSIONS

THE GREAT TURNING

The day has come when Muslim background believers travel the world proclaiming the Gospel among their own co-religionists, just as they are doing at this moment among their own people. The tremendous power pent up in fundamentalist Islam is being transformed into a brave proclamation of the forgiveness of sins through the sacrificial death of the Lord Jesus Christ. In the midst of the turmoil caused by rising fundamentalism God is calling forth his new Sauls to become Pauls or we might say "new Muhammads" to the Moslem people.

Exciting news is coming out of countries where Sunni Muslim Mbbs are winning Shia Muslims to the Lord. Many are paying the ultimate price for sharing the Gospel. The blood of the martyrs, both expatriate and local Muslim background believers, is the catalyst for a great turning of Muslims from every people and tribe to the One that fills their heart's longings. This great turning, once again, is proving the power of the Gospel to save and sanctify.

SELECTED BIBLIOGRAPHY

Isma'il, Adan Ibn, The Belief of Isma'il, Adan Ibn Isma'il, 2003   (iampartners@triconet.org)

Accad, Fouad Elias *Building Bridges:* Christianity and Islam, NavPress, Colorado Springs, CO, 1997.

Adeney, Miriam. *Daughters of Islam:* Building Bridges with Muslim Women, InterVarsity Press, Downers Grove, IL, 2002

Baker, William G. The Cultural Heritage of *Arabs, Islam and the Middle East,* Brown Books Publishing Group, Dallas, TX, 2003

Brustad, Kristen, Al-Batal, Mahmoud, Al-Tonsi, Abbas, *Alif Baa with DVDs, Introduction to Arabic Letters and Sounds,* Georgetown University Press, Washington, DC, 2004

Al-Kitaab fii Ta alum al-Arabiyya with DVDs, A Textbook For Beginning Arabic, Part One, Second Edition

Greeson, Kevin, *Camel Training Manual,* WIGTake Resources, Sudhindra, Bangalore, India, 2004 (customerservice@landforceinc.com)

Hawtmeh, Abdalla with Muller, Roland, **The Man from Gadara,** A True story of Muslims transformed by the power of the gospel, http://rmuller.com, 2003

Hershberger, Mert. *Steps toward Maturity: NT Models for the Stages of Spiritual Growth,* World Christian Foundations: Module 2, William Carey International University (n.d)

Hull, Bill. *New Century Disciplemaking:* Applying Jesus' Ideas for the Future, Revell, Grand Rapids, MI, 1997, 2000.

Love, Fran & Eckheart, Jeleta. Ministry to Muslim Women, *Longing to Call Them Sisters,* William Carey Library, Pasadena, CA. 2000.

Love, Rick. *Muslims, Magic and the Kingdom of God,* William Carey Library, Pasadena, CA, 2000.

Mallouhi, Christine A. *Waging Peace on Islam,* Monarch Books, London, 2000.

Musk, Bill A, *The Unseen Face of Islam,* MARC, Great Britain 1989.

Oksnevad, Roy, *Leadership Development Within the Muslim Background Believer Community,* Unpublished paper for DME 914 Leadership Development and Culture, May 22-June 2, 2006. mmd@wheaton.edu

Pietzsch, Horst B. *Welcome Home,* Caring for Converts from Islam, Life Challenge Africa, Cape Town, SA, 2004

Register, Ray, *Dialogue and Interfaith Witness with Muslims,* 1979, 1995, 2008 distributed by IAM Partners, PO Box 463045, Escondido, CA 92046-3045.

Register, Ray, *Back to Jerusalem,* Church Planting
    Movements in the Holy Land, WinePress,
    Enumclaw, WA, 2000.

Ripken, Nik, *Servants in the Crucible,* Mohit Gupta,
    (http://seebus.ws) January 2005

Stoddard, David A. *The Heart of Mentoring,* 10 Proven
    Principles for Developing People to their Fullest
    Potential, NavPress, 2003.

The Holy Bible (Quranic Arabic) "al-kitaab al-shariyf",
    International Center, B.P. 14, 13080-Luynes,
    France. Email:75102.1246@compuserve.com

The True Furqan, WinePress Publishing, Enumclaw WA
    98022, 1999

Websites

www.answering-islam.org.uk

www.campuscrusade.com

www.PesianMinistries.Org

www.truth-in-crisis.com

www.opendoorsusa.com/

www.christiansincrisis.org/

www.compassdirect.org/

www.persecution.org/

www.jubileecampaign.org/

www.persecution.com/

www.uscirf.gov/

APPENDICES

APPENDIX I

The Seven Muslim-Christian Principles

PRINCIPLE ONE:
God Has a Purpose for Our Lives

PRINCIPLE TWO:
Sin Separates Us from God

PRINCIPLE THREE:
We Can't Save Ourselves

PRINCIPLE FOUR:
The Cross Is the Bridge to Life

PRINCIPLE FIVE:
God's Provision Is a Person

PRINCIPLE SIX:
Making Him Ours

PRINCIPLE SEVEN:
What to Expect When We Accept God's Gift

APPENDIX 2

Beginnings of a CPM among the IAMs

Dr. Ray Register, CPM Consultation
December 4-5, 2003

BACKGROUND

30 years of seed sowing in rocky soil

I served for many years as a field evangelist with the IMB-SBC in Galilee, assisting the Association of Baptist Churches as field representative, but my main interest was in relating the Gospel to Muslims. I tried every method known to man in visitation evangelism with a friend named Ahmad, and with other Muslim friends, to influence Muslims for Christ. Also I spent time training others in this line of work. It took the Lord's timing to see the harvest. If I had left earlier, I would have missed it. As Kenneth Craig indicated in the CALL OF THE MINARET, it is a call to patience. There were some family and local "friends" who thought we should have left much earlier!

The 1st Gulf War, 10/40 Window

God's timing seemed to be, that because of the First Gulf War and Americans and others having to send their boys and girls to the Persian Gulf to fight a war, the 10/40 Window prayer effort took off. I tell people that we got the fallout of these prayers, and not just the Scud missiles! I had been giving tracts and Bibles to a friend who lived in the West Bank and he had been giving them to Arab workers in his town. They started coming to the Lord! He would call me to drive down from Upper Galilee and witness to them in Arabic. Then he would call me to meet him at the Jordan River to baptize them. It seems that the 1st Gulf War and the Iraq-Iran War had formed a crack in the impregnable rock of Islam. Muslims were beginning to open up to options to the obvious violent spirit generated by their religious and political teachings and were ready to hear the Gospel for the first time.

The Church of Samaria

One of the first meetings we held with the Mbbs was in the ruins of an ancient church on Mt. Gerizim near the Samaritan community in Nablus. Therefore the group chose the name "The Church of Samaria." My friend discipled them since he lived in their area, and I encouraged him with advice, visits, and literature. He would often bring them to meetings of other believers for encouragement. One local pastor, an Arab from the USA was very helpful in receiving the Mbbs, and was active in disciplining them and helping them to adjust to the Christian culture.

The "Dirty Dozen" & mixed motivations

I call these first Mbbs the "dirty dozen" since the first 12 believers all came with some ulterior motive, and some fell away, while others remained faithful. They were persecuted, but many stayed with their families and succeeded in winning some of them to the Lord. One young believer who was a Sheikh was run out of his town, but gathered a group in his exile. Another man became an mbb when he found a tract in the glove compartment of a car at a repair garage. His father, an herbal doctor claimed a vision from the Lord. He left his wife and 8 children and married a tourist woman and immigrated to the USA with her. He recently died under mysterious circumstances. Another mbb, a taxi driver was arrested and interrogated in Jericho and eventually fled with his family to our retreat center. We will refer to him later. His cousin became an mbb, but ended up marrying another woman and living with both wives in our city. Several ended up taking new wives, which makes for interesting discipling dynamics! Some were in and out of jail for disputes in their towns with leaders of the political movements in the area. But the common thread is they remained open to contact to hear the Gospel and eventually settled down to a somewhat normal lifestyle.

The move to the center of the harvest field

I kept getting so many calls to travel to the center of the country where the Mbbs were developing that we decided to move there when our rent contract finished on the home in Josephus' village where we were living. A pastor from the Assemblies church who I had taught in his seminary found us a home to rent in his city. It was in a Russian Jewish community and gave us the cover to work with the Muslims since I was an author and teacher. Several of the Church of Samaria group had moved to this city. It was also a crossroad for the Bedouin in their North-South migrations. It is the only city built by the Muslims in the Holy Land during their invasion in the 7th Century and served as their capital until it was destroyed by an earthquake.

The "New Directions" of the IMB-SBC

About this time, in the mid 90's, the IMB-SBC took a radical turn in its overseas approach. They basically eliminated an entire organizational level of field administrators and offered them field positions. They abolished "mission meetings" and organized unreached people group (upg) teams with the goal of reaching the many upgs in the various areas of the world. Borders were no longer the limits for the work. Each team functioned to reach their upg wherever in the world. For the first time they got serious about reaching the many Muslim upgs and were willing to network with other Great

Commission Christian (GCC) groups to get the job done. They asked me to stay on several years past retirement in order to receive training and serve as the Strategy Leader (Coordinator) to catalyze a cpm among the IAMs who were 20% of the population of our country, and numbered about 10 million worldwide. Basically I was given a title for doing what I always wanted to do.

Specialized training for CPM among the IAM UPG

My wife and I were sent to England for intensive specialized training in CPM. I had a BS in Commerce. Much of the training we received could be equated with a MBA. We were taught strategy principles for a CPM, marketing techniques, platforming, Internet research into our upg's culture and awareness of the Gospel, networking with other GCCs, advertising, brainstorming about 100 ways to reach our upg with the Gospel, end visioning, and created a Master Strategy Plan leading to a CPM. This was done in coordination with people on the field who we had recruited to our team. Basically, we were taught that upgs are "messy." When the Lord starts a CPM he does it in ways we may not anticipate. The local men and women of peace need to take the lead in improvising their own strategies to reach their own people using the culturally sensitive approaches that best communicate the Gospel to their own people. That means for the expatriate catalyzer to often take a back seat quickly and let the local Mbbs take over the front-line presentation of the Gospel to their own people. Resources are found in the harvest, in both funding and personnel. We were no longer able to depend on the IMB-SBC for major funding, but were to trust the Lord to provide the needed resources.

End visioning-160,000 Mbbs among the IAMs

In our research we found there were about one million IAMs in our immediate country, 2.5 million in the occupied areas, about 3 million in the adjoining country and another

3.5 million in the worldwide *Diaspora* or a total of about 10 million. If a CPM was to start in our country we would need 160,000 Mbbs to catalyze a CPM, or approximately 16% of their population. This figure has been proven to be a minimum to sustain a societal movement to accept new innovations in most societies. Our End vision therefore included this figure coming to the Lord, and their then influencing their fellow co-religionists to receive the Gospel. I shared this End vision with local GCCs who claimed a vision for our upg when I returned to the country in a closed meeting. One betrayed my confidence and told another GCC about this figure. This man who did not attend our meetings got enraged and put out over the Internet that I was a liar and not to be trusted! He thought I was saying there were 160,000 Mbbs in the country and nothing I said would convince him that this was only a goal and not a statement of reality.

MSP-Master Strategy Plan for implementation

Our Master Strategy Plan contained a step-by-step plan for catalyzing a CPM with the goal set in the End vision. It included goals of evangelism, church planting, discipling, and training with a strong emphasis on platforming and distribution of audio and video presentations of the Gospel and the Jesus Film. Each goal was dated and personnel assigned to lead in the carrying out of the goal, along with other GCCs. All budget requests to the IMB-SBC had to be keyed to this MSP which was approved by our NAME area leadership team. They provided partial resources for materials and projects and we had to use creative means to find the rest of the resources. I was amazed that Episcopals and Catholics were generous in supporting projects, as well as several Parachurch groups.

The IAM Team- ESL Platform

Part of our MSP was to use the platform of English as a Second Language to provide a valued service to the IAM community. We had four volunteers from the USA who accepted the challenge. The first was a Phi Beta Kappa graduate from Kentucky whose aunt and uncle served on another team in our country. She lived with a Muslim family in a key IAM town and taught ESL in the local community center and in surrounding IAM towns. During her two year stay she wrote an orientation manual for future ESL teachers among the IAMs and other Muslim cultures from the perspective of a single woman living with an IAM family. She left us a list of dozens of key contacts for future ESL opportunities. She was followed by a middle aged volunteer from Texas with a winsome personality who lived for a year in an apartment in the same town. She taught ESL in the local schools and followed up many of the contacts of her predecessor. We had another retired male ESL teacher from Florida who lived in a key IAM city about a half hour north who taught ESL during summer school and to the President of the Islamic College in the city. He also taught in a Bedouin town and in another major IAM city. He was of Jamaican origin and was accepted readily due to his dark skin and his mature age. I also had a grandmother from Mississippi and a relative of Elvis Presley with 15 grandchildren who taught ESL in several schools and to children of some of my IAM friends in Galilee. They each left a very positive impact on the IAM communities.

IAM Partners, Inc for prayer and financial support

As part of our MSP for CPM among the IAMs we formed IAM Partners, Inc. as a nonprofit educational charity in the State of California. This allowed non IMB-SBC interested persons and organizations a channel to contribute financially to the needs of the IAM community and to the growing mbb movement. Also it served as a resource for training others in outreach to IAMs and coordinated volunteer efforts of those interested in serving among the IAMs.

IAM Updates

We were encouraged in our CPM training in England to form

a network of prayer partners for the spiritual warfare needed to open hearts to the Gospel among the IAMs. This network has now grown to over 700 prayer partners, many of whom share the IAM Updates with friends and other Email prayer networks. The total effect is several thousand people praying for our upg. IAM Updates are usually short, timely prayer updates which are generic. We do not give out names or locations of Mbbs or workers. Those needing explanation are supplied with a set of keys to unlock our terms.

IMPLEMENTATION

A failure that led us to our "Man and Woman of Peace"

The taxi driver I mentioned earlier was finally released from his interrogation by the Secret Police and fled with his family to our retreat center. After a year he moved to our city. I helped to raise rent for his house and made the first (admitted) mistake of my career. I gave him the check rather than to the landlord. The next day he fled back across the border to his home village and spent the money finishing up his house! (He later died in prison.) But before he left, a friend who had been helping him sneaked my telephone number off his mobile phone and called me. This friend whom I call "Barnabas" told me, "I was once married to a Christian woman in Beirut. She used to take me to the Orthodox Church. I could not understand anything. I want you to teach me how to be a Christian, how to live with my wives as a Christian, how to raise my children as Christians, and how to fast and pray as a Christian." So begins the saga of Barnabas and Lydia.

Barnabas and his three wives and three packs of cigarettes a day!

When Barnabas came to us he had three wives. (He said, "Don't criticize me. We can marry four at one time, but you Christians just marry them one after the other!) He at that time smoked three packs of cigarettes every day; I assume one for each wife! His oldest wife lived across the border in occupied territory and was very sickly after bearing him eight children. She was about to die, so we prayed for her and she got well! She and her adult children in the major cities across the border became believers. His second wife who lived in the territory to the south was a fundamentalist and divorced him. He had to scramble around and scrape up her "mohar" or dowry, under orders of the Muslim court in our country, because he had become a "kafir." Her oldest daughter who was in high school became a believer and began finding teachers who were secret believers in her school. His youngest wife, who we will call Lydia, held out the longest. Her brother was a Sheikh and beat her up and kicked her out of her family home when she finally confessed Christ. His two oldest sons became believers and led many of their friends to the Lord.

The Hook and the Bait

Two of the simple witness and discipling tools we used besides the Bible were a no- smoking tract in Arabic from South Africa called, "The Cigarette Talks." Most Arabs in our country smoked heavily and I told them it was America's secret weapon to kill them all! So the no-smoking tract was very popular among the young people and adults. At the end of the tract it says the only person who can get you unhooked from the smoking habit is Jesus. Then we used the Four Spiritual Laws in Arabic, which we revised, with permission, to have one law on each page. I led Barnabas to confess the Lord using the "Four" and he began using it to lead other IAMs to the Lord.

Released to baptize others

I agreed to disciple Barnabas on condition that everything I taught him he would pass on to others. He would call me to give a friend the Four. I did it one time and the next time he called I told him to give them the Four. I baptized him. One day he called me and said there are a number of young men up in the hills who have accepted the Lord and want to be baptized.

But if he has me baptize them they will be hauled in by the Secret Police, interrogated and possibly imprisoned. So, I told him to baptize them! He said, "Can I?" I said, "Of course." If you need help let me know and I will instruct you over the phone. For a while we were in danger of forming a tradition of traveling to the Jordan River for baptisms. But that got too expensive, so he started baptizing them in local streams, springs and even bathtubs. The movement began to grow.

Women coming to the Lord

A student volunteer doing a summer project for a Christian college left a Bible with the leader of a woman's club near Abraham's town. The leader died several years later and Barnabas conducted our first mbb funeral in her home. The local sheikhs had gotten angry and left because there were so many Mbbs present and Barnabas led her funeral service using scripture I gave him over the mobile phone.

Lydia, his youngest wife, who he now lives with, became a dynamic evangelist. She witnessed to her family who were spread over many of the key towns and cities of the occupied territories. One day Barnabas asked me if it was alright for Lydia to baptize the women since it was difficult for him to baptized women who were not from his family. I said, "I am not sure we Baptists do it that way." He said, "Then you better get used to it because we are!" Lydia was able to go places where Barnabas could not go for security reasons, and the women's movement took off. Several of her sisters became strong believers and their children started a student movement in the local universities.

Student movement-scholarships and a martyr

The mbb students began to meet for Bible study on the campus of a University in Abe's town. We had about 10 students on small scholarships through grants given by a parachurch organization. Our stipulation was that they were Mbbs and nonsmokers. Their group grew so large that it began to intimidate the leading Muslim fundamentalist movement on campus. On one occasion the secretary of the University who was a friend had Barnabas come on campus to lead a *sulha* or reconciliation between the competing groups. Then, during a violent demonstration on campus, the leader of our student movement was dragged out of the office where he and other Mbbs were taking refuge. He was stabbed as a "kafir." He became our first martyr. Altogether we had at least three Mbbs killed in violence between the occupation army and local citizens.

Outreach through audio cassettes resulting in demands for J Film- 450 new Mbbs

A GCC partner church in England sponsored a tape distribution project utilizing a Gospel Recording church planting tape in Arabic along with the Wordless Booklet. This was received well, especially by the Bedouin. We recorded about 450 Bedouin and other IAMs who were baptized as a result of the widespread distribution of the cassettes and wordless booklet. The distribution of audio cassettes generated a demand for the Jesus Film video in Arabic. As part of our MSP we planned to distribute over 100,000 Jesus Films in Arabic, one for each IAM home in the country, as resources became available. The tape project was coupled with food distribution from another GCC partner for needy Mbbs suffering from being excluded from the food relief of Muslim organizations.

Burnings, beatings, destruction, more martyrs and a growing movement

As the movement of Mbbs grew among the IAMs and their PAM relatives across the border, so grew the intensity of persecution. Barnabas had several cars damaged. Other believers had their windshields smashed. One group of Mbbs in a village started a kindergarten. It was burned several times along with the home of the mbb leader. His son was run down on the highway and required intensive medical treatment. Barnabas was burned all over his face by a fire bomb. We learned to caution Mbbs from the beginning to be wise in their witness until they could win their families and neighbors to the Lord. In several locations security personnel who became Mbbs protected the other Mbbs.

The believers supported each other emotionally when their unbelieving wives refused to sleep with their believing husbands. Using patience many of the wives accepted the faith of their husbands. They usually did not introduce an mbb to other Mbbs for several months until they could be sure they were sincere and would not betray the other Mbbs to hostile opponents. Two of Barnabas' daughters were divorced by their husbands who went back to Islam, mainly because of financial need.

The near fatal staged accident and the 25 to make 1,000!

As a result of the successful tape distribution project, Barnabas was enticed out late one stormy night by a call from a supposedly distressed mbb. Both Lydia and I warned him not to go, but his shepherd's heart overcame our warnings. He and his driver noticed a car following them when they got to a lonely stretch of road. The car forced them off the road. Their vehicle overturned several times, leaving Barnabas severely injured with 6 broken ribs. I left him in a coma in the major hospital in the Land when I returned to the States for my final furlough in April of 2000. While he lay unconscious in the hospital for a month the Mbbs he had led to the Lord baptized 25 new Mbbs to bring the movement over the 1000 mark. They have shared the Gospel also with their Christian, Druze and Jewish friends.

The Society of Light Charity- for the Mbbs, recognized by the government

Before we left the country we assisted Barnabas and other Mbbs to form a nonprofit organization which could raise financial aid for scholarships, relief and other projects for the

Mbbs, and also provide a means to enlist volunteers for ESL and other projects in the future. The Society of Light Charity was recognized by the government. Its operation is monitored by the Government office of nonprofit organizations and its books audited regularly. It acts as the sister organization to IAM Partners, Inc. Volunteers who followed me have assisted in the bookkeeping and relating to donor organizations.

THE ONGOING AFTERMATH

Multiple discipleship centers

As a result of outreach of Barnabas and Lydia and other Mbbs associated with them, about 50 centers have been established in homes and communities throughout the country and the occupied territories. Some number only a few Mbbs whereas others now have 50 or more baptized believers in their town. The tense security situation has made it difficult to keep up with numbers but the information we have is they continue to meet and break bread together in similar fashion to the early church. They sometimes attend Christian Arab churches in their communities and Evangelical conferences when the security situation permits.

Believers baptizing believers

Our goal in discipling Barnabas and Lydia was that they would disciple others. They have created their own discipleship materials in Arabic which has been more suited to their needs than the western created materials we provided in the beginning. For instance, he said that the Four Spiritual Laws is too much meat for a new mbb in the beginning. He created two or three levels of discipleship material before and after the level of the Four. On several occasions I would come with ideas and materials for discipleship and leadership training and would find he had already created culturally sensitive materials in Arabic from his own experience and resources. In general they took a non-confronting approach to their Muslim friends, often using the Quran as a bridge to the Gospel. They used Mazhar Malouchi's commentary on Luke and also the True Furqan with some effectiveness among fundamentalist Muslims. We visited a number of Evangelical churches and they chose the one that suited the believers best for Bible training. One was pastored by a believer of Druze background who helped disciple Barnabas through a Bible correspondence course. The new leadership developed under them baptized other Mbbs when the security situation allowed, but often called on Barnabas or Lydia to assist them.

Continual struggle for project finances

With my leaving the country, project finances have gradually fallen off. Difficulties with accounting and language and cultural barriers between donors and the Society of Light Charity have caused a ceasing of most of our project funding. This has been very difficult on Barnabas, who contrary to my warnings, and to the grief of Lydia has borrowed money on several occasions for food relief and scholarships. This indebtedness has placed a heavy strain on his family. We are still on a learning curve on this matter. But he has declared to me that he has learned his lesson and will carry on no projects unless funds are available. The Mbbs have shared each others burdens on occasion, so the need now is to bring available resources in line with the practical needs of the mbb groups and the opportunities of outreach. What amazes me is these people who have been through literal fire, broken bones and recurring poverty (some self-generated!) keep on for the Lord. I expected many times for them to return to Islam since the Muslim leadership often approaches them with fistfuls of money to pay their debts if they will turn back to Islam.

New team members

We continue to encourage a handful of volunteers to the IAM team who try to encourage Barnabas and Lydia and the other Mbbs in their outreach. There is great opportunity for trained, culturally sensitive volunteers to encourage the Mbbs. We have maintained a separation between volunteer activities and the work of Barnabas and Lydia and the Mbbs. The expatriate volunteers add value to the community while the Mbbs work behind the scenes to reap the harvest.

A White Harvest

What I have related concerning the IAM team is being repeated in several other locations in the land with other GCC partners, indicating that despite the volatile political and military situation and the near poverty of many of the Mbbs, there is a real hunger for the Gospel among the Muslims of the Holy Land. Pray that the Lord would send forth laborers into this white harvest, both from the right kind of expatriates and from among the mbb harvest.

Dr. Ray Register, Director IAM Partners, Inc.
raysmore @cs.com

APPENDIX 3

Sensitivities In Discipleship Of Middle Easterners
Ray G. Register Jr. And Fredrick Wedge
November 17, 1979
Cyprus

"The aim of our charge is love that issues from a pure heart and a good conscience and a sincere faith." I Timothy 1:5

Sensitivity is based on love, not on sentimentality. Love is based on the supernatural work of the Holy Spirit, issuing from a pure heart cleansed by the blood of Christ, a heart that does not bear prejudice against those of different religions and cultures.

A good conscious is one that does not harbor suspicion or grudges from the past.

A sincere faith is one that is not threatened by opposing beliefs or customs.

All are prerequisites to discipling Middle Easterners whether Muslim, Druze, Jews, Catholics, Orthodox.

My emphasis will be on those of the Muslim faith.

Sensitivity is a unique quality of being able to get inside another persons heart and to feel as He or she feels, to respond from our own feelings and experiences, and to allow God to draw us together in love and understanding.

It requires a high level of Personal security, which is a supernatural gift of the Holy Spirit. Not every pastor, teacher or missionary is capable of such sensitivity. It will not be possible for you or me to disciple every person we know. But at least we can be aware of some of their feelings and direct some gifted person to relate to that person so he may be discipled.

Discipleship is intensely personal, especially with Muslims.

It requires our time, energy, and emotions. Most of us are not engaged in discipleship, but in pre-evangelism or follow-up.

Discipleship means a personal relationship that is more than holding a class for new converts. I am not an expert in discipleship. Many of you have much more experience. My experience is more with pre-evangelism and apologetics, the defense and proclaiming of the faith to Muslims. I have made many mistakes.

So you will have to forgive me if I disappoint you today. At least I will try to share a few ideas gathered from my limited experiences and from Muslim and Christian friends who have helped me to understand this subject better. Discipleship-Sharing a life, in order that he also may share this Life with others.

Who are we discipling?

1.   Inquirers- seekers after truth. Those who are troubled, puzzled, looking for direction. God has sent them our way for a reason. They feel our love and our sensitivity to their need. They crave friendship and trust. They are like sick persons who feel a need and a deep discontent, who come to the hospital because they feel the hospital has a possible diagnosis and cure for their need. They are not sure about their illness, but they know that what is troubling them is not being cured in

their present situation. They fear death. They sense the joy and peace of the resurrection life in you and desire it for themselves, though they fear it. (Cultivating)

2.   Believers- These have found the cure to their hearts yearnings in Jesus Christ. They have been healed and now want to know how to go back and live in a sick world. Will the world cause them to get sick again or can they overcome?

I.   The First step in being sensitive in discipling Middle Easterners is to:

Know their background

1)   His personal life - his home life, work situation, personal conduct with friends, religious background, emotional stability, what others think about him. His fears, failures, habits, and talents. Feel with him, first as a fellow human being.

Second, as a person of a particular cultural and religious background. Then, as a fellow sojourner on the path of faith. If we are going to be equipped to disciple Muslims we must have at least read the Ouran through, and know a minimum of church history and the heresies.

It will help you to be sensitive to the Muslims problems with certain ideas that we hold dear. It will help you to feel the spiritual attacks he is enduring as He seeks a deeper faith in Christ. It will aid you in correcting many misconceptions and prejudices. Much that the Muslim holds against the Christian faith is not based on the Quran or the Bible, but upon tradition. You must know the difference in order to avoid controversy over non-essentials.

2)   **His fears and Prejudices**-some stem from lack of Peace - he is afraid. His world could be shattered if he discovered that all his life has been built on a **half-truth**! Your

own spiritual struggles should help you to be sensitive to this. This is why **personal testimony is valuable in discipleship**. Particularly if he is a new inquirer- **his apparent pride and toughness is a cover-up for a lack of Peace. He is afraid.** History has reinforced his fears-Muslim Christian polemic has sharpened his arguments. The Crusades and Middle East conflict has convinced him of the injustice of the West of which you as a Christian or missionary are a symbol. What can you do to help him in overcoming his background and grow in faith in Christ? How can you avoid arousing his fears?

a)   Maintain the ideal of a loving, faithful, loyal friend so as to gain and maintain his full respect. Be the kind of person he can imitate. He is so unhappy, so lacking in peace that he is looking for it everywhere. He is a very fertile field for growth, but he is covered with a **hard covering of fear**. Unfortunately many Christians have not experienced the depths of love that can penetrate this covering of fear. Many of us need the radical spiritual surgery of the Holy Spirit in order to let the love flow out.

The story is told of the father who took his daughter with him to the subway. While waiting for the train they were surprised to see police guarding. Then the police brought a famous criminal into the station to transport him to prison. The little girl wanted a closer look. She looked into the criminal's face and saw the saddest expression. She returned to her father, remarking, "I did not mean to make him so sad!" Then she went over to the criminal and told him, "I did not mean to make you so sad! Please forgive me. I love you and Jesus loves you too. "Later when the criminal had been in prison several weeks the warden said to him, "You certainly are not the hardened criminal the newspaper wrote about!" He answered, "You are right, I am new man ever since a little girl expressed her love to me. That is the first Time in my life anyone ever loved me!"

If the Christian reveals his love he might instigate in the Muslim's mind the question, "How come you are so happy and full of peace?" So, avoid arousing his fears by being a true friend, a loving friend he will desire to imitate.

b)   Do not debate with the Muslim as to the goodness or badness of his faith. Do not make him feel you are superior to him, or that you disdain him or his people. Show him at least that you are in love with the truth and wisdom and would like to hear some of his "truth and wisdom." This requires much patience. Create a situation that will make him say, "Well let us hear some of your truth and wisdom. My experience is that the Muslim expects and desires to hear about our spiritual knowledge. **Silence is a sign of agreement or weakness**, or can arouse suspicion of what we are doing.

I fear though that Christian education, in churches and schools in the Middle East has unconsciously developed or reinforced a spirit of pride in the hearts of some Christians that has deepened prejudice between Christian and Muslim. We must speak the truth in love to the Muslim and not wield it as an intellectual sword.

Admit that you **yourself have had questions** about matters of theology and doctrine, but after study, prayer and experience, with logic, you are convinced that your faith is right for yourself and that it gives you joy and peace

II.   How would a Muslim believer counsel and caution us in discipling the Muslim inquirer?

These are some brief guidelines from a Muslim friend who is anxious that we know the way to share the truth of Christ with other Muslims.

1.   Accept, admire, and love the Muslim as Your true friend.

Challenge him to accept people as they are, so that he

may ultimately acquire such a great heart and a wise mind that he can take in all people, and all situations without prejudice. We will be expecting too much to think that he will immediately acquire a perfect Christian life. (There are quite a few Christians who have also failed at this!) He will need teaching, encouragement and occasional rebuke as he grows in his understanding of Scripture and the life of God in Him.

Remember- He needs a model to imitate, someone who points him daily to Jesus. A Muslim friend calls me several times a week and says, "Pray for me". I cannot refuse such a request! Another Muslim friend prays for me every day, and for my children. So I am getting more than equal return on my prayers!

   2. **You do not have to completely uphold the same political or social views of your Muslim friend**.

It is the mistake of some Christian missionaries and even Christian nationals to overcompensate for the fact that they are not Muslims. They become more fanatical than the Muslims in Religion and politics! Some missionaries I have heard of are thinking of becoming Muslims in order to win other Muslims. Instead, show him that you are sensitive to his bad lot, and to the mistakes of those responsible for the policies he suffers from.

Avoid making him or them feel they are absolutely right in a stand or cause, but let him know that you understand he does have a cause that needs an answer. He has to come to see eventually that the will of God and the cause of Christ have ultimate priority over social and political problems.

   3. If you can be of any help in a problem or difficulty he will always be grateful and loyal to you.

The Muslim always lives in difficulties and problems, like all people. By being sensitive, wise and helpful you may sow love into his mind and heart, and some member of his family, preferably some young would-be enlightened person. Never **forget that all his family is watching you and listening to you.**

Do not harden your heart against him. Remember, he was not responsible for his birth into a religious system that has made him so resistant to the Gospel.

When a true believer makes a promise for help he will *[must]* always honor that promise because it is a part of his faith.

4.   **The best place to create the best atmosphere for making the Muslim listen to you easily and comfortably is outside his own home, community and environment.** Remember, his greatest fear may be the ridicule and threats of other Muslims, and even unwise and insensitive Christians. It is Preferable to meet with him in the privacy of your own Christian home where you can be open and non-artificial.

(The Muslim will test you at this point to see if you really trust him to visit in your home and to be around your wife and daughters! We practice discretion even as Americans at this point. Our women should be neither naive nor over-cautious.)

A saying of Muhammad goes: "Know one another, and you will love one another. Visit one another, and you will love one another. Exchange gifts with one another, and you will love one another."

Always keep an eye open on a fit member of the family to encourage them to enter a Christian school or enterprise in personal life, so that the Word may be sown in his heart

The Muslim will never forget the favors you do for him or a member of his family.

5.   A Muslim wants above all for his secrets to be well kept.
Be sure you never let him down in that matter in any way because of his psychological and social fears. Do not spread his name around even among believers without his permission. It is healthier for his spiritual growth that he does his own testifying about his experiences with the Lord. He could be put in real danger and embarrassment, particularly if he is trying to stay with his family and society.

Introduce him only to Christian friends who can be trusted. In our Joy for his new faith we may be unwise in spreading the word about him too easily. He knows when the time is right. Trust the Holy Spirit to reveal this to him, and hope he can influence hundreds of others for Jesus.

6.   Is it better for him to stay in his own environment or to replant him in another environment until he is strong and able to stand opposition? Perhaps in another location he can grow and attract others around him, better than in his home situation. If he is weak and immature he could be snuffed out by the hate of those who oppose his new faith. **This is a question that needs to be decided by the situation and the person involved.** Maybe it is best to bring a strong Muslim believer from another country to live and witness among your people. Take away the Muslim's fears by assuring him that his questions will be answered objectively and treated with secrecy, and you will not refer to him as a Christian believer, on a record or document, and only outside his environment with his agreement.

7.   **Be a model of faith and honesty for him to emulate.**
Be honest and faithful. (Be a new Muhammad to Him, a faithful follower of Christ). Be wise in dealing with him, be

strict in morals but loving and forgiving. Have the spiritual sensitivity of a shepherd be soft, simple, and non-benefiting. Say "No!" to him with the deepest regret. Share his life, sit with them, eat with them, cry with them! Remember, discipleship is sharing a Life! Not just teaching about a life.

III.   Now in closing, what are some of the basic spiritual guidelines for sensitive discipleship of a Muslim believer, or any other believer for that matter?

1.   **Help him to know the faith.** That means the difference between religions and denominations, and real faith in God through Christ. Fourteen years visiting a village - Mukhtar thought I believed in the Pope! Let him   see that the New Birth is essential, that the Holy Spirit has been born anew in his heart through the work of Jesus on the Cross.

2.   **Let him know the cost of discipleship.** It means his whole life laid on the altar for Christ. Help him to see the cost of God's love- for his sins, the death of Christ the Lamb of God for his personal sins. Isaiah 53 – I have seen Muslims weep. With this the burden of forgiving others- this may be the greatest burden. Keep the cost before him, so in times of testing he will not feel you have deceived him. He will know the great price God has paid for his sins and it will inspire him to grow strong and brave in Christ. (Also wise!)

3.   **Know the difference between being tempted and backsliding.** Every believer is tempted. Testing will strengthen his faith as he learns to overcome through the supernatural power of Christ in him. Backsliding comes when he fails to count the cost of total commitment, and begins to regret what he left behind. Be sure that what YOU are requiring of him comes from Christ and not just from your "Christian" Culture. The New Testament is always the ultimate authority and not the teachings of a particular denomination.

4.   Teach him the Power of Christ over the Devil and his demons. Islam is influenced by the occult, incantations (ihjaab), and will fire the fiery darts of the evil one at the new believer. **Be sensitive to his dreams, visions.** The Muslim has a deep mystical instinct. Let him see the power of prayer in healing, and the wise use of the gifts of the Spirit. Muslims are sensitive and responsive to the power of prayer.

5.   Encourage him to witness wisely to his family and friends and to live a life in keeping with his witness. Some emotionally unstable Muslims believers have created their own persecution and rejection from their family and other believers. One burned himself with kerosene. Some of these people need wise and careful counseling and perhaps exorcism of tormenting and disturbing spirits.

6. Use the Scripture and prayer at every occasion. He is hungry for spiritual nourishment. Just as he praying Muslim washes himself before prayer, the believer in Christ washes his mind and heart with the written Word of God before prayer. It is inward but it requires outward action.

7.   Let Baptism be his decision. Leave it up to him as whether it should be "Private" or public. There is no such thing as "secret" baptism when another person is present! Again help him to count the cost. It is his relationship to Christ that counts. The Holy Spirit will lead to wisdom in this matter. Philip did not call the church council down from Jerusalem to baptize the Ethiopian. "Secret Baptism" with several trusted believers present is not secret! We need to restudy baptism as a personal commitment to Christ.

CONCLUSION

What can the church do to receive new Muslim believers and enable them to grow?

1. Have a sensitive person in your fellowship trained to work specifically with Muslims. Perhaps he can develop a small fellowship of Muslim inquirers that can be incorporated into the church as they are ready. It will take time for the church to get ready also. The Muslim believer can tell you those who he feels are sensitive to this type of ministry.

2. He will seek out on his own the real believers from his Muslim friends. This will result in a chain reaction, a "secret" society of friends of Jesus, who study the Bible and pray together, who marry their children to one another. The Spirit of Jesus who is most sensitive to the Muslims heart will lead them. Do not fear if this fellowship grows outside the walls of your local church. As long as you, the trusted and sensitive Christian friend are involved, the link with the local church is there, for the church is not the building but, the fellowship of true believers. Many will prefer to worship away from their home environment for obvious reasons until there is true freedom.

Train interested members in outreach to Muslims.

Finally, Let us not fear the rise of radical Islam, but be sensitive to see it as the cry of the human heart, enslaved by humiliation and fear, for the love, joy, and peace that only Christ offers. Pray for the supernatural work of the Holy Spirit, that brings us into the family of the one true God.

-- Ray G. Register Jr. November 17, 1979, Cyprus

APPENDIX 4

VMMP Conference, Burnoby, BC. Canada
1 November 2003

MEETING THE NEEDS OF MBBS
IN NORTH AMERICA
G. Stevenson — Many Paths Lead to Christ?

1. Read Gospel story.
2. See Jesus in dream or vision.
3. Struggle with evil spirits — find name of Jesus frees them.
4. Abused or in dysfunctional relationship — *greater power in Jesus.*
5. Long for justice in society and find this in Jesus.
6. Desperate for freedom from immoral lifestyle.
7. Fearing death and longing for assurance of paradise.
8. Women find *that* Jesus affirms them.
9. Since a child, longed for intimacy with God and finds in Jesus.
10. Because family has decided to join.

Nonetheless, Jesus must become the "issue" that colors their mental landscape, the one who captures their heart.

Their Unvoiced Questions of You
1. What do you think of me? — issue: love — or, "Can I *trust* you? Are you safe? Do you care?"
2. Do you have deeply held convictions? — issue: spiritual passion — translated, "Are you a person?"

3.   And do you live by these convictions? — *issue:* integrity — or "I may not like your views, but can I respect you?" i.e., Is there consistency in what Jesus says and we do?

What Do They Need from Us?
First considerations: A "cookie-cutter/turn-key" approach will fail. Do you care for him/her? Are you listening? Don't do it alone. Are you working with others and in an accountable relationship with a mentor or coach? *Above all, no technique will ever replace your intimate walk with Christ. You cannot give what you do not have.*

1.   Prepare them for and coach them through hardship resulting from their new faith. Every new believer needs a family; they've lost theirs — rejoice and grieve with them (Mark 10:29-30).
2.   Teach how they may relate Christ to weak areas of life: revenge and forgiveness, lies, fear, bribes and dishonest business practices, honouring parents, and physical and emotional abuse (forgiveness releases effects of abuse).
3.   Affirm their value — their intelligence and character have been belittled — let them know you are committed to them.
4.   Demonstrate and teach on real love — giving, not taking; memorize 1 Corinthians 13 — and model loving marriage and family.
5.   Teach about spiritual warfare, how to resist powers used against them.
6.   Encourage and support them to keep from compromise or lying and strengthen them when they fall.
7.   Help them establish a pattern of basic spiritual disciplines, such as prayer, Bible reading and meditation, especially in their own language and in culturally appropriate ways.

8.   <u>Develop support network of friends</u> willing to help find work, housing, legal advice, etc.

9.   <u>Introduce to stronger Mbbs</u>, especially from their own ethnic group, for fellowship and mentoring.

10.   <u>Teach basics of faith</u> — through story, rather than expositional format.

11.   <u>Help them discover and develop</u> their spiritual gifts and leadership abilities.

12.   <u>Support them through difficult teachings of Scripture</u> — e.g., unsaved family members lost.

13.   <u>Coach them how to *wisely* disclose their new faith</u> to family and friends — without pressuring how soon they do so.

14.   <u>Respect beliefs and give time and space to respond</u>; expect growth in knowledge and grace (Philippians 3:15-16).

What Should Our Objectives Be?

1.   MBB churches with MBB leadership, reaching out to unsaved Muslim immigrants of their own ethnic background.

2.   Demonstrate value for the individual MBB by aiming at one-on-one ministry more than groups and *classes,* and by giving lots of time to individuals.

3.   Take Mbbs with us as we model evangelistic and discipleship ministries in order to push Mbbs forward in ministry and leadership from the beginning.

4.   Canadian churches' main function should be as mother churches <u>facilitating</u> the establishment of MBB ethnic fellowships and churches.

5.   We must develop support networks to meet the needs of MBBs in times of crisis.

Note: The numbering format above does not reflect any order of priority.

Sources

1.   MBB's Life in North America. Workshop notes, presented by Georges Houssney & Richard Bailey at COMMA III Conference, Chicago, IL (October 2003)

2.   From Fear to Faith. Compiled by Mary Ann Cate & Karol Downey. William Carey Library Publishers, Pasadena, CA. (2002)

3.   Ministry to Muslim Women: Longing to Call Them Sisters. Edited by Fran Love & Jeleta Eckheart, William Carey Library Publishers, Pasadena, CA. (2000)

APPENDIX 5

The C1 to C6 Spectrum

A Practical Tool for Defining Six Types of '"Christ-centered Communities" ("C") found in the Muslim Context

The C1 -C6 Spectrum compares and contrasts types of "Christ-centered communities (groups of believers in Christ) found in the Muslim world. The six types in the spectrum are differentiated by language, culture, worship forms, degree of freedom to worship with others, and religious identity. All worship Jesus as Lord and core elements of the gospel are the same from group to group. The spectrum attempts to address the enormous diversity which exists throughout the Muslim world in terms of ethnicity, history, traditions, language, culture, and in some cases, theology.

The diversity means that myriad approaches are needed to successfully share the gospel and plant Christ-centered communities among the world's 1 billion followers of Islam. The purpose of the spectrum is to assist church planters and Muslim background believers to ascertain which type of Christ-centered communities may draw the most people from the target group to Christ and best fit in a given context. All of these six types are presently found in some part of the Muslim world.

C1—Traditional Church Using Outsider** Language
May be Orthodox, Catholic, or Protestant. Some predate Islam. Thousands of CI churches are found in Muslim lands

today. Many reflect Western culture. A huge cultural chasm often exists between the church and the surrounding Muslim community. Some Muslim background believers may be found in C1 churches. C1 believers call themselves "Christians."

C2—Traditional Church Using Insider** Language

Essentially the same as C1 except for language. Though insider language is used, religious vocabulary is probably non-Islamic (distinctively "Christian"). The cultural gap between Muslims and C2 is still large. Often more Muslim background believers are found in C2 than C1. The majority of churches located in the Muslim world today are C1 or C2. C2 believers call themselves "Christians."

C3—Contextualized Christ-centered Communities Using Insider Language and Religiously Neutral Insider Cultural Forms

Religiously neutral forms may include folk music, ethnic dress, artwork, etc. Islamic elements (where present) are "filtered out" so as to use purely "cultural" forms. The aim is to reduce foreignness of the gospel and the church by contextualizing to biblically permissible cultural forms. May meet in a church building or more religiously neutral location. C3 congregations are comprised of a majority of Muslim background believers. C3 believers call themselves "Christians."

C4—Contextualized Christ-centered Communities Using Insider Language and Biblically Permissible Cultural and Islamic Forms

Similar to C3, however, biblically permissible Islamic forms and practices are also utilized (e.g. praying with raised hands, keeping the fast, avoiding pork, alcohol, and dogs as pets, using Islamic terms, dress, etc.). C1 and C2 forms avoided. Meetings not held in church buildings. C4 communities comprised almost entirely of Muslim background believers. C4 believers, though highly contextualized, are usually not seen as Muslim by the Muslim community. C4 believers identify themselves as "followers of isa the Messiah" (or something similar).

C5—Christ-centered Communities of "Messianic Muslims" Who Have Accepted Jesus as Lord and Savior

C5 believers remain legally and socially within the community of Islam. Somewhat similar to the Messianic Jewish movement, aspects of Islamic theology which are incompatible with the Bible are rejected, or reinterpreted if possible. Participation in corporate Islamic worship varies from person to person and group to group. C5 believers meet regularly with other C5 believers and share their faith with unsaved Muslims. Unsaved Muslims may see C5 believers as theologically deviant and may eventually expel them from the community of Islam. Where entire villages accept Christ, C5 may result in "Messianic mosques." C5 believers are viewed as Muslims by the Muslim community and refer to themselves as Muslims who follow Isa the Messiah.

C6—Small Christ-centered Communities of Secret/ Underground Believers

Similar to persecuted believers suffering under totalitarian regimes. Due to fear, isolation, or threat of extreme governmental/community legal action or retaliation (including capital punishment), C6 believers worship Christ secretly (individually or perhaps infrequently in small clusters). Many come to Christ through dreams, visions, miracles, radio broadcasts, tracts, Christian witness while abroad, or reading the Bible on their own initiative. C6 (as opposed to C5) believers are usually silent about their faith. C6 is not ideal; God desires his people to witness and have regular fellowship (Heb 10:25). Nonetheless C6 believers are part of our family in Christ. Though God may call some to a life of suffering, imprisonment, or martyrdom, He may be pleased to have some worship Him in secret, at least for a time. C6 believers are perceived as Muslims by the Muslim community and identify themselves as Muslims.

*A pseudonym.

** "Insider" pertains to the local Muslim population; "outsider" pertains to the local non-Muslim population. John Travis (a pseudonym) has been involved in planting congregations among Muslims in Asia for the past 12 years.

He is currently working on a Ph.D. through an American university. Used by permission from "The C1 to C6 Spectrum," *Evangelical Missions Quarterly*, 34:3 (October 1998), published by EMIS, P.O. Box 794, Wheaton, IL 60189.

APPENDIX 6

The Jericho House Group Lessons
From the Jesus House of Prayer, Terry McIntosh, 11/02
USAJOURNEY@aol.com

BORN AGAIN

Lesson # 1 Born Again lesson.

Explain purpose, educate, why we follow Jesus, many promises, benefits, a safe way for all.

According to the history of the Arab peoples, al-Kindi was the thinker with whom the history of Islamic philosophy virtually began. He said, "We should not be ashamed to acknowledge truth from whatever source it comes to us, even if it is brought to us by former generations and foreign peoples. For him who seeks the truth there is nothing of higher value than truth itself."

(John 3: 1-2)

One evening, under the cover of darkness, a religious teacher went to Jesus. He had been watching Jesus and listening to him in the city. But he did not want his peers to know that he was interested in the message that Jesus was preaching. He said, "Teacher, we know you have come from God. For no one could perform the miraculous signs you are doing if God were not with him."

(verse 3-4)

Jesus then said something that confused this respected teacher of God's Law. Jesus said, "I tell you the truth, no one can see the kingdom of God unless he is born again." The religious teacher asked, "How can a man be born again when he is old? Surely he cannot enter a second time into his mothers'' womb to be born."

(Jesus answered in verse 5)

Jesus was not speaking in earthy terms, but in spiritual terms. The religious leader was still thinking in earthy terms and did not understand things of the spirit. All of us are earthy, from the earth, and think and reason along earthy understandings. Jesus wanted to take us from the earthy realm to the spiritual realm. This is a very important step for all of us because He said, "no one can see the kingdom of God unless he is born again."

From the earthy understanding, Adam is the father of all men. All nations and people groups have descended from him. When asked who is our father, many will say "Adam". This is true. But once we are born again as Jesus said we must be, we begin to think in spiritual terms rather than earthy terms.

Once we accept God's plan to save us, we are welcomed into His family and become sons and daughters of God by the Spirit of Adoption. God becomes our "Father". It is in the spiritual sense, of course, since God does not have natural children. We become as brothers and sisters in the eyes of God and are a part of His worldwide family.

Jesus wants to raise our level of awareness about spiritual issues. If we remain earth bound in our thinking, then we will never come into a full relationship with God as He wants us to do. Things of the earth, including our fathers, die and pass away. Things of the Spirit are eternal and much more important.-

Pray to be born again. Ask God to send the Holy Spirit of Truth to be with us and lead us into all truth. Pray for the peace of

Jerusalem and for the other groups.

HG #2 Who is the family of God?

Recap last week's lesson about being born again with spiritual insight and understanding. "You must be born again." Remind of goal to educate and benefit. Think in spiritual terms.

God creates spiritual families: (Matthew 12: 46-50). Jesus was not denying his responsibility to his earthly family. On the contrary, he criticized religious leaders for not following the Torah command to honor their parents. Jesus was pointing out that spiritual relationships are as binding as physical ones, and he was paving the way for a new community of believers, our spiritual family.

Called God's sons: (Romans 8:13-17.) Adoption as sons illustrates the believer's new relationship with God. In Roman culture, the adopted person lost all his rights in his old family and gained all the rights of a legitimate child in his new earthly family. He became a full heir (equal) to his new father's estate. Likewise, when a person becomes a disciple of Jesus, he or she gains all the benefits and responsibilities of a child in God's family. *One of the benefits is being led by the Spirit. We may not always feel like we belong to God, but the Spirit is our witness. His inward presence, in us, reminds us of who we are and encourages us. As God's children, we share in great treasures as equals. He has already given us his best gifts. Jesus, forgiveness and eternal life and the right to ask him for whatever we need.

The Koran agrees. It says, Surah 3 (Imran) v. 54 (pg. 147). There is benefit in knowing Jesus and following him. Surah 3, v. 44 confirms a special place for Jesus. (pg.142). If someone believes the Koran, they are obligated to follow Jesus.

Who is not a son or daughter of God? (John 8: 31-47).

v. 31, those who hold to Jesus teachings are real disciples.

v. 36, Jesus is the truth that sets us free. He is the source and perfect standard of what is right. He frees us from hell, self deception, and from deception by Satan and men. He shows us the way to eternal life with God. Jesus can break the evil power over you and your life.

v.41, the religious leaders were hereditary children of Abraham via Isaac, and claimed to be sons of God. But their actions showed them to be true children of Satan for they lived under Satan's guidance. True children of God would not act like they did. Going to the mosque or church does not make you a true child of God. Your true father is the one you imitate and obey.

v.43, the religious leaders were unable to understand because they refused to listen. Satan used their stubbornness, pride, and prejudices to keep them from learning the truth and following Jesus.

v.44-45, the actions of these leaders identified them as followers of Satan. They did not realize it, but their hatred of truth, their lies, and their evil hearts showed how much control Satan had over them. They were tools of Satan. Satan uses people today in the same way.

v. 46-47, Jesus welcomed people to challenge his claims and character, but wanted them to follow through with what they discovered. Many people never challenge Jesus to see what is true. Others test him but are not willing to believe what they learn. If we refuse the truth about Jesus, we cannot be real children of God. God's children love Jesus and hold to his teachings.

Next week, we will learn more about who he is so that we can make the right connection and start getting the benefits. Ask questions, pray.

HG # 3 " Introducing the Big Brother"

Recap: How must we see things (with spiritual eyes) (Who is our Father?)God is the Father of all who follow him in truth. (What is most important to our Father, religion or people?)

God creates spiritual families made up of people from all backgrounds. Religion is supposed to help, not control. (Who does Jesus say we are if we hold to his teachings?) Jesus calls us his brothers and sisters.

(Reaffirm God's love and concern for women in general. In the Hadith, Muhammed said, "I have seen hell, and the most of them are women. "Refute as untrue. More women follow God than men. Many women followed Jesus. It does not have to be like Muhammed said. Stress equals before God thru Jesus with all the same benefits.)

This week we learn more about Jesus Himself. Who did Jesus say sent Him to earth? (God- John 7:16, pg. 293). Why did God send Him? (To make a safe way for us- John 14:6, page 321) What is his relationship to God?

(He is a reflection of God- John 12:44-46, page 317) Is he the Son of God? (Yes, Luke 1: 35, page 166). Expound.

The Koran says that God has no children. What does that really mean? Education plays a very important role in understanding this. (Explain.)

Historical facts are that a small group of people called Marinites worshipped the Sun and stars and the planet Venus. When they heard about Jesus, they tried to follow but included their pagan religion. They started believing that God had sex with Mary and produced Jesus.

Muhammed was combating that heresy. Christians also denounced it. The sect died out in about 100 years. So actually the Koran is correct in saying that God does not have a son in the natural sense. However, we are talking about a special spiritual relationship. No Christians believe that God had sex with Mary. Uneducated religious teachers and those who love a lie, have twisted the facts to make Muslims think otherwise.

Some Islamic teachers say the Injil has been changed. But that is only because they do not understand what they read, and they do not know the history. They are not educated about the facts, so they make a very serious charge against God. The Koran says in 6:34 that the word of God cannot change, and 10:64 confirms that. The Koran says that the Injil is light in 5:46, and Allah told Muhammed to ask the people who have the Injil if he had any questions in 10:94. It is dangerous to deny the words of God! If someone professes to believe in the Koran, they must accept that the Bible is the genuine word of God.

Jesus is revealed in the Injil, not the Koran. If He did it once, why would God have to do that again in any other book? The Injil is where we meet Jesus and God's plan for mankind.

If the Injil had been changed, God would have warned us. It is only men who say it. The Injil was already in circulation around the world, and it was an impossible task for anyone to change one word without getting caught. Those who claim it has been changed are just trying to run away from some difficult things they don't understand. They never present proof of any change, just wild stories.

They are not in God's family because they do not love the truth. They love religion, but not the truth. They are just like the Jewish religious leaders in Jesus'' time. The Koran says believers in the Book (Injil) are doing right. (Koran 2: 177, page 71). There are variations of Islam, and only one will be saved. Which one? The one who does what is right! It is most important to follow the true way.

The real meaning of the word Islam is Submission to God, not submission to religion. So, do we believe the Injil has been changed or not? (Make sure of understanding before proceeding)

Jesus is also the High Priest of God's family. (Heb 6: 16-20.-Forever). The Koran says Jesus has a special place of honor and his followers will be above the others. (Koran 3: 45 & 3: 54). Jesus lived 600 years before Muhammed and was appointed as High Priest then. God did not change his mind 600 years later. He is not like a man who changes like the wind. If one says he believes in the Koran, then he must start looking at Jesus as the High Priest.

Why is it important to follow Jesus? (Because he is a reflection of God, he represents truth, and because he makes a safe way for all of us. Early followers were called "followers of the Way.")

Do we want to follow Jesus or not? We will learn more about Him next week.

Pray collectively and for individuals. Ask, " Who is Jesus" . Reaffirm what the scriptures say. Take questions. Be patient. Repeat basic facts often to be sure they are understood.

HG #4 "The Cross"

Stop at each point and affirm understanding. We have learned several things. (1). Religion is supposed to serve us, not control us. (2). God creates spiritual families and he is the Father of all those who follow him in the right way. (3). God sent Jesus to make a safe way for all of us. (4). Jesus is a reflection of God in the flesh, he is the Way, the Truth, and the Life, and the Son of God. (5). Jesus is our big brother and the High Priest of God's spiritual family. (6). We cannot be in God's family and bypass the Son. We have to adhere to God's chosen authority and agree with God. (7). If God is not our Father, the devil is!

Today, we are going to examine the most important part of the gospel. That is the death, burial, and resurrection of Jesus. But first, we need to understand the role of a High Priest. Islam and Christianity both have priest. (EXPOUND ON RELIGIOUS PRIESTHOOD). The office of priesthood is meant to serve the people, not the people serve the priest.

Sin had to be punished because God is a holy God and will not live with sin. He has to punish sin or he would not be a **just** God. Since life is in the blood, God decreed that blood had to be spilled to pay for the sin. (Heb. 9: 22, pg. 666) God permitted the sacrifice to temporarily atone for the sins of the people, but he was never satisfied with the blood of goats and animals. An animal sacrifice would always be temporary, and the High Priest had to continue making sacrifices on behalf of himself and the people every year. However, God had planned all along to send someone to pay the price forever just at the right time in history. His **mercy** made a way for justice to be accomplished. He chose Jesus to serve as the High Priest who would make a permanent sacrifice that would satisfy God's punishment of sin (Heb. 5: 1-5, pg. 654). God said that EVERYONE who accepts this permanent sacrifice becomes a permanent member of his family and has no fear of hell. (Heb 5: 15, pg. 665). The sacrifice is permanent. (Heb 5: 27-28, pg. 667). His blood makes us perfect before God (Heb. 10:11-14, pg. 668). It was God's plan to save us, and Jesus was willing to go to the cross so that his perfect blood would pay the penalty of our sins. (Example: Jesus is like a rope that pulls us up to God.)

Islam teaches that Jesus did not die on the cross. Mish Mazboot! (That is not right!). The Koran testifies to the fact, but some teachers have twisted the meaning of words because they do not understand or do not love the truth. If someone claims to believe the Koran, they should accept what it really says and stop playing with its words! We must hold on to what is good and true and throw away everything else that proves to be false, whatever that source may be.

(EXAMINE KORAN). It is said that Jesus predicted the order of his life, birth, death, and resurrection (Surah 19: 33, pg. 600) "Peace on me the day I was born, and the day I die, and the day I am raised to life." This agrees with the gospel and remember the Koran verse in Surah 3:54 where God said, "I will cause you to die..." A Hadith says that Jesus did not die, was taken to Heaven alive, will return, live 40 years, and then die. Because of that, teachers switch what is supposed to be the words of

Jesus. He said he would die first. Teachers say he was raised up first. They also say the word "die" means sleep, but that is inconsistent with reality. If the Koran is from God like they say, why are they twisting its words? (Remember that Islam split into different denominations just 40 years after Mohammed died). It is also written in the Koran that Jesus said he died (Surah 5:117, pg. 276) (BE PREPARED TO EXPLAIN IN DEPTH).

The real problem. (Surah 4:157, pg. 230). Koran says they did not crucify him nor killed him, he was made to appear like it. If this is true, then you should throw the Koran away right now because it contradicts itself and cannot be the word of God! How can Jesus die and then God deny it 600 years later? This is madge-noon. (crazy). I would not serve a god who could not remember what happened yesterday.

(CLOSE EXAMINATION OF FACTS). According to Islamic scholars, the word "ma salabu-hu" in Surah 4:154 does not negate Jesus being nailed to the cross, but his having expired on it. The words shubbiha la-hum has 2 meanings - "he was made to be like it", or to "resemble it".

Uneducated teachers made up a story that someone who resembled Jesus was put on the cross in His place. This is a widely held belief, but is one of the biggest lies in history! There is no evidence to support it, and cannot be born out in the Koran as true. It is just a story. If the Koran is to be consistent and in line with the Bible it supports, there has to be a better explanation.

Let us suppose that the Romans and Jewish religious leaders thought that Jesus was finished because the body died. However, he lived in the spirit because he is the Spirit and Word of God which cannot be killed. This is the only reasonable explanation that keeps the account in order. God cannot truthfully say that Jesus died in one place and deny it in another place. Jesus said he died, he did not say he went to sleep. (Sleep in the bible, however, was also used for death).

This agrees with the Injil account of his death, burial, and resurrection. Anything else is just wrong.

If the word "die" in surah 3:54 has two meanings as some suggest, then we have an option to choose which one is correct. If we translate the word into "sleep", this denies the whole story as reported in the Injil, which the Koran confirms as right. That makes for many troubles within the Koran itself because Jesus said he died in Surah 5:117. If we translate the word "die" as "die", then the story is consistent with the Injil account. I don't think Mohammed intended to change the story on purpose. No one else should either.

None of us will ever completely agree on the mysteries of God because none of us will ever fully comprehend them. But this is one issue that we must agree upon - Jesus died for our sins on the cross! If we deny this truth, we are calling God a liar and trampling on the blood of Jesus Christ! We cannot call God our Father if we call him a liar and refuse Jesus. Jesus said that if we disown him, he will disown us! (Matt.10: 32-33, pg. 30).

No body ever spoke like Jesus did. He was perfect in example, conduct, and worship. Jesus lived every word he spoke. But we cannot, that is why we need his help. I want my big brother, the great High Priest, speaking up for me on judgment day!

Next week we will learn about the resurrection and the next step in making the right connection.

Take questions, be patient, repeat key points, pray for spiritual revelation to go along with intellectual knowledge. Pray for truth to prevail and a personal visitation for each person from the Holy Spirit sometime this week.

HG# 5 Saints
This weeks HG lesson is for the purpose of salvation. I am sharing this fomat with you so that you will know what is being said and how it is being handled. The El Kaderi group will be

on #4, but everyone else is getting this message on Tuesday, Thursday, and two groups on Saturday.

Please pray for the Truth to prevail, for the Spirit of Revelation and Salvation over these ladies.

Thank You.

HG #5 The Decision

So far we have learned some very important things about the family of God. We have learned more about Jesus and his place in the family as the Son and the Great High Priest. We have learned that we cannot get to God unless we go through Jesus because He is the Way, the Truth, and the Life.

Last week, we learned that Jesus actually died on the cross. If we do not accept God's testimony about this, there is no need to go any further. This is a point we all must understand and agree to if we are to be a part of God's family. The HS will work out the many details, but God's true children are not deceived by the words of men and do not call Him a liar!

Today, we are ready to start a new life in God through Jesus. I talked about the treasure chest of God, and said that Jesus is the key to it. It is full of good things for us. Jesus said, (explain background prompting the statement; natural food vs. spiritual food) ""I am the Bread of Life...."(John 6:35-40, pg. 289). Examine each verse closely. Eternal life is the first free gift we take out of the treasure chest! Emphasize EVERYONE.

Our only other option is to live a perfect life without sin because God will not live with sinners. I used the example of me being a perfect man, but one morning saw a beautiful woman walking down the street and I lusted for her in my heart. I lusted so strongly that I followed her into the street. My heart was breaking God's laws. A taxi came around the corner of the street, hit me, and I died. I died a lawbreaker after having lived perfectly up until then. Since God will not live with lawbreakers, I am cast into hell. Jesus is the safe way. It is a promise to all who follow him.

Jesus also said, ""I am the living bread....my flesh...for the world."" (John 6:51, pg. 290).

Remember to use our spiritual understanding, not the natural. He was talking about dying on the cross for our sins. He went on to say, (John 6: 57-58, pg. 291). Eternal life is a promise from God because Jesus paid the penalty for our sins if we accept this great act of love. On judgment day, God will find many sins in McIntosh. He will say, "Barra!" (Get out!). But my big brother and Great High Priest will put his arms around me and say, "Father, McIntosh is with me. I paid the penalty for him." The Father will then say, "Welcome." Once we realize what Jesus is doing for us, we cannot help but love him more and more! (Cite examples of forgiveness in the Bible) Eternal Life is the first benefit of our relationship with God through Jesus Christ.

When God raised Jesus to life on the 3rd day, it was for a reason. Islamic teachers do not know the reason and miss all the benefit. We need a living High Priest who understands us. Dead people do not help us. If they did, let's go to the graveyard and start praying. There is a reason that Jesus is alive. He is able to help us in many ways.

The resurrection from the grave was a demonstration of God's power over death. It is proof of life after death. It is also proof that God is greater than Satan. Satan wanted to destroy Jesus. He cannot. God has given Jesus power over Satan. The resurrection also represents new hope for all of us in many ways, including safety from Satan. It is evidence of God's sovereign control over life and death. We are promised to live forever if we accept the One who made it possible for us.

(Explain facts surrounding resurrection; important for the natural thinking Muslim; Roman guards would have been executed for sleeping, 500 witnesses, etc.) God did not take

Jesus to Heaven to escape the cross as some say, but sent him to go to the cross for everyone! It was a sacrifice of love.

The next step is to accept this sacrifice of love. It is a personal choice everyone must make.

Read (John 3: 35-36, pg. 278). Today is the day of salvation. Are you ready? Do you believe God''s testimony about Jesus? Do you believe that he died on the cross for our sins and God raised him to life on the 3rd day? Do you believe that Jesus is Lord? Are you ready to admit that you are a sinner? Are you ready to give up religion as your savior?

If so, then it is God who has given you the understanding and you can make sure of your salvation right now. The Bible says, (Romans 10:9-13, pg. 472). The Bible also says, (Acts 2: 38-39, pg. 351) Correctly, the translation should read, "Repent and be baptize because your sins have been forgiven." When we repent, Jesus baptizes us with the Holy Spirit. (Illustrate: You are in the ocean, under and completely surrounded by water, totally immersed, it fills your lungs. So it is with the Spirit that comes to live in us.) We are never alone from that moment on! He is with us! We will learn about water baptism and its significance soon. (requires a trusted female presence.)

If you do not believe this, do not say so. God knows the heart anyway. But if you do believe it, I want you to forget about everyone else for a moment. Do not think about them. Think about yourself and what is best for you. No one here can help you on judgment day. This is between you and God. This is very personal and very important.

You can say it in a lot of ways, but I am going to pray with you as an example. I will ask you now to follow this prayer if you believe God''s testimony about Jesus. (Lead prayer).

Close with congratulations and encouragement.

Explain that the HS of Truth will now lead us into a deeper relationship and continue to reveal God's plan for us. Now that we have the key, the treasure chest is open to us. Next week, we will look inside!

Pray for continued revelation and a sense of well being and peace for each lady. Take questions. Repeat key points. Express joy at their decision to follow Christ.

HG #6 New Life-(Where to Start?)

Recall commitment to Lord Jesus. Encourage. (continue meeting together), study, learn. Emphasize family and LOVE!

Open treasure chest. First gift is eternal life. Second gift, although part of the first, is the Holy Spirit. Mention various purposes of HS. Promised to pour out His Spirit.(Acts 2: 17, 18, pg. 349)

Seals us (Eph. 1: 13-14, pg. 571). Jesus said is with us and in us (John 14:15-17, pg. 322), never leave (Heb. 13:5, pg. 680). Use ocean example.

Told to be filled with HS (Eph. 5:18, pg. 579)=Produces change, (compare to getting drunk) = Jesus sends the HS ""streams of living water"" (John 7: 37-39, pg. 295).

Gives hope (Romans 15: 13, pg. 483)

Brings Power (and victory) over Satan, etc. Was and is involved with every aspect of God. From creation, to birth of Christ, miracles, etc.

Gives us what to speak, comforts, teaches, removes burdens (Acts 15: 28-29, pg. 397), always present. Does not speak on his own, but the words of God.

Sin against (Matt. 12:32)

We must remain in Jesus. (John 15, pg. 323 , read and explain).

Intro water baptism in more detail and explain difference between Spirit and water. (Acts 19:1-7, pg. 410). Spirit saves, water demonstrates.

It originated with an early Jewish custom of baptizing converts to Judiasm. John baptized with water, Jesus with the Holy Spirit. Water baptism was carried over as a tradition and pledge of good conscience to God. Cornelius and family were baptized in the spirit first (Acts 10:44-48, pg. 381). It is not a black and white issue. When one understands it and is ready to demonstrate the inward change via water baptism, then is the time.

Close with prayer for filling of HS as promised to all believers and offer prayer of salvation to any new faces. Appeal to God for the baptism of the Holy Spirit.

Take questions.(Time did not permit explanation of water baptism this week).

HG Lesson #7

We have come a long way in a very short time. If you have accepted Jesus, your future is secure and you are ""holding the master key in your hands."" Jesus is the one who unlocks that treasure chest of God for us. We already have the gift of eternal life and assurance that the Holy Spirit is with us and in us. This is very important to know, think about, and remember at all times

In my absence, I have prepared a series of lessons that will help you. Please continue to meet together. Nasser will be here and Tony and Marium will also visit and pray with you.

Today''s lesson is about prayer. It is our lifeline (telephone) to God. It is His chosen way of hearing from us. The whole Bible emphasizes the willingness and ability of God to answer prayer. (Matt. 7: 7-11, pg. 18). God is more willing to answer prayer than we are to pray. However, in order to receive the answers to our prayers, we must meet the conditions stated in God's word.

We ask in the name of Jesus. (Recall John 14). There is a reason we do that. He sent the Holy Spirit to us so that God''s power can work in our lives. God gave him the authority to send the Holy Spirit to those who follow him. The promise is only for the disciples of Jesus.

A religious Muslim friend said that God will not listen to my prayers because I do not follow requirements defined by Islam. Islam requires you to wash your arms and face and ""clean"" yourself up on the outside. Islam teaches that when you follow the prescribed prayer ritual of Islamic confession and bowing several times, then you will get God"s attention. My friend is mistaken because he does not understand the things of the Spirit and has to rely on ""outward"" appearance and action. At best, rituals serve only as a temporary, repetitive attempt.

It is for freedom that Christ set us free! (Gal 5: 1, pg. 566). That means a lot and it includes freedom from the demands of religious rituals. You have God"s permission to go straight to him from your heart in the name of Jesus who paid for your eternal safety and brought you into the family. We are not bound by religious traditions!

EXAMPLE:
Imagine a family where the children are required to clean up their rooms and put on clean clothes before their father will listen to them. This is madgnoon (crazy)! There would not be a lot of conversation in that family.

But in a real family where love abounds, the children are al-ways talking and yelling "Baba" (Dad)! They run directly to their father because they know he loves them and will listen. They also know that he will do the very best for them at all times. This is one of the many benefits we take out of the treasure chest. The disciples of Jesus are permitted to go direct to God in prayer at any time, anywhere, for any reason and He promises to listen! (Repeat) The Holy Spirit is only given to those who follow Jesus. The promise is not for everyone.

We must have the right attitude and character. We should praise God, give him thanks and praise. We must worship him in spirit and truth (John 4: 24, pg. 280) in righteousness and obedience. These things are possible only as we live in Jesus, the true vine. Our motive must be pure and for God''s glory, not ours (James 4: 3, pg. 691) and we must trust God (James 1: 6-7).

Pray according to God''s will. (I John 5: 14-15, pg. 726) with faith. Pray regular and with persistence (Luke 18: 1-8, pg. 237). Pray together (Matt. 18: 18-20, pg. 58). Believers prayer example (Acts 4: 24, pg. 356). Go to the closet when praying alone, do not make a show and depend on rituals (Matt. 6: 6-8,pg.14).

Lord''s Prayer (Matt. 6: 9-13, pg. 15). Expound. Not limited to repetitious prayer, just example.

We must have the supernatural help of the Holy Spirit to do these things, but we have direct access to the heart and ear of God! You will learn many more things over the next few weeks, and you will also learn how to ""hear"" from God. Prayer is the God chosen method of making our wants and wishes known to Him. It is a special privilege through Jesus only.

Close with corporate and individual prayer. Take questions.

APPENDIX 7

Servants in the Crucible

A biblical missiology of suffering
that leads to witness and church planting
in the midst of persecution and martyrdom

In 1991 there were approximately 150 Somali followers of Christ among the 8 million Somalis in the Horn of Africa. By 1997 these 150 believers had been reduced to 4. Followers of Islam systematically hunted down these believers and those they did not kill were forced to flee to other countries.

While those killed were followers of Jesus, the timing of their deaths was more related to outside, Western influences in their lives than with being a positive Christian witness to the Somali Muslims surrounding them. They were killed for whom they worked and for whom they went weekly to share worship. They were killed for possessing literate copies of the Bible and other discipleship materials though they lived in the midst of a highly illiterate population. Also, they were killed as they were paid to evangelize in locally inappropriate manners.

From this experience rose a number of godly thoughts and initiatives, embracing the global mission enterprise. There arose a deeply held conviction that "when" persecution comes, not "if" it comes, let it be for who Jesus is and not for the outsider. This experience led the authors of Servants in the Crucible to visit 60 countries, interviewing approximately 600 believers, for whom persecution is normal. These brothers and sisters have taught us much, those of us in the West, about biblical suffering, persecution and martyrdom as they partner with witness and church planting.

These interviews have led the authors to develop a 3-4 day workshop that assists believers globally, and the church locally, to develop a biblical missiology of suffering. The goal is not simply to highlight suffering, persecution and martyrdom. The goal is a bold biblical witness and the planting of the New Testament church in the midst of environments defined by persecution. Such a workshop offers

- Compelling stories of faith within environments of persecution
- In-depth training for those who serve in the midst of persecution
- Training for those churches and agencies who would send missionaries as "sheep among wolves"
- Tools for witness and planting house churches at home as the nations come to our doorstep
- A clear view of what the Father is accomplishing among the nations
- A missiology of suffering that calls us to faith and continued service even when Satan attacks and kills "our" fruit
- An opportunity to see the Bible come alive as the Father makes Himself known among the nations in glory and power.

To download Servants in the Crucible go to http://seebus.ws. When you get online, enter user name: casa and password: Pd49ex. Workshops can be booked by emailing Nik Ripken at < Nripken@attglobal.net>. This is a pen name that the missionary uses for security purposes. Feel free to share this website.

The author and his wife, natives of Kentucky, are 21-year veterans of the mission field. Currently they live in Ethiopia and serve as Strategy Associates for Northern Africa and the Middle East. In the past two years these workshops have been utilized in 14 countries internationally and numerous settings in the USA. The workshops are often sponsored by seminaries and church-based colleges for credit. Yet our focus remains getting this material within local churches and sending bodies that send their sons and daughters to the nations. There is no charge for leading these workshops other than transportation to and from wherever we might be. Hospitality that includes food and a room would be appreciated.

In the US and the West, these workshops enable pastoral staff, denominational workers, sending agencies and lay leaders to embrace suffering as normal, partnering with the God of heaven where He works and how He works. Churches that have hosted a workshop have substantially increased and deepened their going and sending to the nations. Often their giving to mission causes has double and tripled.

This material attempts to place its fingers on the pulse of God as He moves in the midst or persecution and martyrdom.

ABOUT THE AUTHOR

Dr. Ray G. Register, Jr. (BS, MDiv, MA, DMin) became acquainted with Muslims as a student at the University of Virginia in 1953. He served as a Southern Baptist Representative to Arabs in Nazareth and the Arab villages of Galilee and Palestine, ministering among the Arabic speaking people of Israel and Palestine for nearly 40 years. Dr. Register designed a guide to Dialogue and Interfaith Witness with Muslims with the help of his Muslim friends. It was field tested as a project of ministry among Muslims for the Doctor of Ministry degree in the USA.

Dr. Register is a native of Columbia, South Carolina, grew up in Charlotte, North Carolina and was educated at the University of Virginia, Hartford Seminary Foundation, The Overseas School of the Hebrew University in Jerusalem on Mt. Scopus, and the Southeastern Baptist Theological Seminary. He taught Arabic and Middle East studies at Southeastern Baptist Seminary as a visiting professor and served as an adjunct professor at the Southern California Campus of the Golden Gate Baptist Theological Seminary. He directs IAM Partners, Inc., a nonprofit educational charity dedicated to advocating the educational and spiritual needs of the Muslims of the Holy Land and worldwide.

Ray and his wife, Rose Mary (Rich), continue their lifelong ministry discipling Middle Eastern believers. They have three grown children, five grandchildren and two great-grandchildren. For comments, further information about this book, or inquiries about needs and opportunities among the Muslims of the Holy Land write, FAX or email to:

IAM Partners, Inc.
970 W. Valley Pkwy # 185
Escondido, CA 92025-2554
FAX: 1-760-480-8063
iampartners@triconet.org

Discipling Middle Eastern Believers
ISBN 978-1-935434-36-8

TAKE A NEW LOOK AT A CLASSIC IN THE FIELD OF COMMUNICATING WITH MUSLIMS

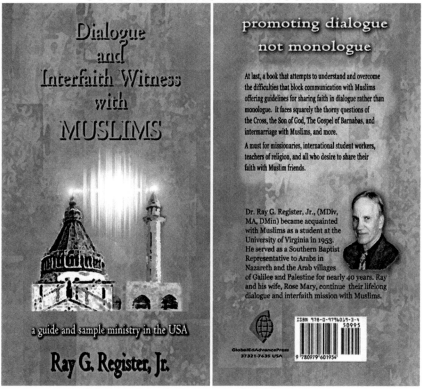

Dialogue and Interfaith Witness with MUSLIMS

a guide and sample ministry in the USA

Ray G. Register, Jr.

promoting dialogue not monologue

At last, a book that attempts to understand and overcome the difficulties that block communication with Muslims offering guidelines for sharing faith in dialogue rather than monologue. It faces squarely the thorny questions of the Cross, the Son of God, The Gospel of Barnabas, and intermarriage with Muslims, and more.

A must for missionaries, international student workers, teachers of religion, and all who desire to share their faith with Muslim friends.

Dr. Ray G. Register, Jr., (MDiv, MA, DMin) became acquainted with Muslims as a student at the University of Virginia in 1953. He served as a Southern Baptist Representative to Arabs in Nazareth and the Arab villages of Galilee and Palestine for nearly 40 years. Ray and his wife, Rose Mary, continue their lifelong dialogue and interfaith mission with Muslims.

ISBN 978-0-9796019-3-4
50995

GlobalEdAdvancePress
37321-7635 USA

9 780979 601934

$9.95 [ ] ISBN 978-0-9796019-9-6
DIALOGUE AND INTERFAITH WITNESS WITH MUSLIMS

At last, a book that attempts to understand and overcome the difficulties that block communication with Muslims, with guidelines for sharing faith in dialogue rather than monologue. It faces squarely the thorny questions of the Cross, the Son of God, the Gospel of Barnabas, and intermarriage with Muslims, plus many others. This book shares the common ground needed to overcome the communications barrier with Muslims. A must for missionaries, international student workers, teachers of religion, and all who desire to share their faith with Muslim friends.

AVAILABLE AT WWW.GLOBALEDADVANCE.ORG,
Barnes & Noble.com; Amazon.com; among others or
Order from the author: Dr. Ray Register,
P.O. Box 463045, Escondido, CA 92046-3045,
760-294-2114 Home & FAX
or direct email: raysmore@cs.com

CPSIA information can be obtained at www.ICGtesting.com
Printed in the USA
BVOW05s0618280214

346272BV00008B/169/P